GARLIC Garlic *Garlic*

Recipe ideas using the world's supreme herb

GARLIC Garlic *Garlic*

Recipe ideas using the world's supreme herb

Edited by Lydia Darbyshire

CHARTWELL
BOOKS, INC.

A QUINTET BOOK

Published in 2004 by **Chartwell Books**
A Division of **Book Sales, Inc.**
114, Northfield Avenue
Edison, New Jersey 08837

This edition was produced for sale in the U.S.A., its territories and dependencies only.

ISBN 0-7858-1787-5

This book was designed and produced by
Quintet Publishing Limited
6 Blundell Street
London N7 9BH

Creative Director: Richard Dewing
Art Director: Clare Reynolds
Design: Giles Ellis
Project Editor: Toria Leitch
Editor: Lydia Darbyshire
Illustrator: Shona Cameron

Material in this book previously appeared in: *The Great Chile Pepper Cookbook*, Gina Steer; *The Real Chile Bookbook*, Marjie Lambert; *Korean Cooking*, Hilaire Walden; *Mexican Cooking*, Roger Hicks; *Indian Low-Fat Cooking*, Roshi Razzaq; *Thai Cooking*, Kurt Kahrs; *Stir-Fry Cooking*, Bridget Jones; *Creole Cooking*, Sue Mullen; *The Great Garlic Cookbook*, Sophie Hale; *Pickles, Relishes & Chutneys*, Gail Duff; *Mexican Main Dishes*, Marlena Spieler

Typeset in Great Britain by
Central Southern Typesetters, Eastbourne
Manufactured in Hong Kong by
Regent Publishing Pte Ltd
Printed in China by SNP
Leefung Printers Ltd

The Publisher wishes to thank the following for permission to reproduce the illustrations:
p. 7 and 9 Casecross Ltd; p. 8 ET Archive Ltd.

CONTENTS

INTRODUCTION 6

SOUPS AND APPETIZERS 10

SNACKS AND SAVORIES 42

PASTA AND GRAINS 66

FISH AND SEAFOOD 84

MEAT AND POULTRY 100

VEGETABLES AND SALADS 130

PRESERVES, SAUCES, AND DIPS 162

DRINKS AND DESSERTS 182

INDEX 192

INTRODUCTION

Garlic has always been more than just a flavoring. In the course of its long history it has been worshipped by the Greeks and the Egyptians; it inspired the first recorded industrial strike; it has had binding oaths sworn upon it; it has been used as hard currency, to ward off the plague and the evil eye, and to diagnose pregnancy; and it was reputed to cure anything from cancer to thinning hair. It has also been used to preserve meats and corpses,

to temper steel, to provide vigor on the battlefield and in bed, and to keep pests from crops and vampires from virgins.

Without doubt, garlic (*Allium sativum*) is one of the most versatile plants there is. Its botanical name derives from the Latin word *allium*, which means odorous, and it is one of more than 300 species within a genus that includes onions, leeks, scallions, shallots, and chives. The word garlic itself derives from two Scandinavian or Norse words, *gar,* meaning spear, and *leac,* meaning a leek, which are clearly references to the plant's tall, slender stalk.

Most people would regard garlic as the strongest tasting vegetable, certainly the strongest of the entire onion family, with its sulfureous, pungent taste. However, that need not be the case, for, cooked carefully, the effect can be as powerful or as subtle as you wish. The quantities recommended in the recipes in this book, therefore, are not necessarily reflected in the strength of the final result. A chicken stuffed with 40 cloves of whole, blanched garlic and baked in a low oven will not be nearly as garlicky as a chicken served with an aïoli (raw garlic sauce) made with an eighth of that quantity.

Some people are afraid of smelling of garlic. Parsley, chlorophyll preparations, absorbents such as peas and beans, and other breath fresheners will help. But why worry? Garlic smells like good food; bad breath is bad breath.

Garlic can be rubbed around a salad bowl or fondue pan, or crushed or finely chopped and fried over a high heat to give a strong flavor to sauces for pasta and grains.

GARLIC IN THE KITCHEN

When you buy garlic, make sure that the bulbs are firm and well filled out, and that there are no tears in the outer sheath. The skin of the bulb can be papery white, pink, or purplish, depending on where it was grown and at what time of year you buy it. But the flavor will vary little. If you want to keep it, store it in a cool, dry place.

A garlic press is useful if you use garlic a lot. Plastic is best, although you can use a stainless steel or even a wooden one. Bruise the clove lightly to loosen the skin, then crush it, unpeeled, collecting the juice and pulp as it comes through the holes. This makes cleaning the press a lot simpler: just pick out the skin and rinse the press in hot running water.

As the smell of garlic tends to linger, it is a good idea to keep a chopping board specifically for garlic and onions, and to wrap garlicky food in an airtight bag and waxed paper before placing it in the refrigerator or freezer.

GARLIC IN THE GARDEN

Although garlic can be bought all year round, it is easy to grow. It is hardy, but does need a period of heat and sun while it matures. To plant, carefully separate the cloves in a garlic bulb and plant them, except the two or three in the center, 1½ inches deep and about 6 inches apart, pointed end up. If you are planting a lot of garlic, leave about 12 inches between the rows. The soil should be fertile but fine and well drained. Planted in early spring, the garlic will be ready to harvest in fall, when the foliage will have turned brown and started to shrivel. If the bulbs are planted in mid-fall, the garlic will be ready the following summer. Loosen the earth around each bulb with a fork, and be careful not to tear open the sheaths when you lift out the bulbs. Dry the garlic off in the sun or in an open shed, and shake off any loose soil. The bulbs can be strung together and stored in cool, dry conditions until they are needed.

Garlic can also be grown in rich soil in pots on a sunny windowsill. Plants the bulbs at a depth of 1 inch. Pots kept indoors near a source of heat should be well watered from the bottom. This also humidifies the room.

You can also grow garlic from seed. Several varieties can be bought from seed suppliers and garden nurseries, and you will probably find a wider selection of varieties than if you simply grow from bulbs. The seed supplier will be able to advise you on the best type to choose and the best way to cultivate it.

GARLIC IN HISTORY

The smell of garlic has permeated history for at least 6000 years, and even longer if you take the Moslem view that when a triumphant Satan left the Garden of Eden, onions sprang from his right footprint and garlic from his left. Garlic is believed to have originated in the Siberian desert, been brought to Egypt by way of Asian nomadic tribes, and from there back up through India via the trade routes to eastern Asia, then west to Europe. It was carried by Phoenician traders and Viking sailors, who believed it would fortify

(left) Garlic chives growing.

(right) The Indian woman is using a large sieve to separate the garlic cloves from the loose outer skins.

them on their journeys and help them to treat any illnesses that struck on the voyage.

For all these cultures, whether Indian or Egyptian, Babylonian, Greek, Russian, Hebrew or Chinese, garlic was almost as important an element of their daily lives as salt. Had the Roman ruling classes been less snobbish about the pungency, we might now be receiving an "alliary" instead of the (salt-derived) salary. In ancient Egypt, 15 pounds would buy a slave, and, until the middle of the eighteenth century, the Siberians paid their taxes in garlic.

A fourteenth-century illustration shows how important garlic was medicinally at this time, even if its culinary use was limited.

By the time of Horace (65–8 BC), garlic was frowned on by upper class Roman households, although it was consumed by the mass of people in great quantities. Garlic was especially popular with the army, who planted it wherever they went, and it soon became a symbol of military life.

Marco Polo (1254–1324) recorded that the Chinese used garlic to preserve raw meat and to detoxify—and disguise the taste of—any meat that had gone off. The Egyptians used it as part of the mummification process and buried it with the dead. Six cloves of garlic were found in Tutankhamen's tomb, while painted clay models of garlic bulbs have been discovered in pre-pharaonic burial sites, put there to ward off any evil spirits that might impede the soul's journey to the afterlife. Bodies found in Theban tombs wear necklaces of garlic for much the same reason.

Garlic's protective powers against malign spirits—especially the evil eye—also applied to the living. In modern Egypt there is still a festival known as "sniffing the breezes" during which garlic is eaten, worn, and smashed on doorframes and windowsills to keep malignant forces at bay.

Wherever it was popular, garlic was a class indicator, soon spurned by the upwardly mobile, the aristocracy and, in some cases, by the clergy, but enthusiastically embraced as food and physic by the masses, causing the French author Raspail to call it the "camphor of the poor." Such snobbery could prove fatal: during an epidemic in 1608, visiting French priests could comfort London's sick with no ill-effects, due to the garlic they ate, while many of their English counterparts died.

GARLIC IN FOLKLORE

Garlic is probably best know, outside the kitchen, as a vampire repellant. In Bram Stocker's Dracula (1897), the Dutch vampire expert Abraham Van Helsing makes Count Dracula's intended victim, Lucy, wear a wreath of garlic flowers, and he rubs them around the window, door, and fireplace of her bedroom as the first line of defense.

The Saxons of Transylvania in central Europe, the very heart of vampire country, would stuff the mouths of suspect corpses with garlic before burial. A few cloves kept in a money bag were believed to keep witches from your gold and, hung in dairies, to stop supernatural interference with milk production. If you gave garlic away, however, the "luck" would go with it.

Throughout antiquity, garlic was regarded as a protection for those vulnerable to the evil eye—virgins, newborn infants (no Greek midwife would attempt a delivery without a good supply of garlic to hand), engaged couples, and newly weds. Indeed, anyone could be subject to malign influences at some time or another, and if the worst should happen and no garlic were to hand at a potentially hazardous moment, a loud cry of "Here's garlic in your eyes!" was believed to do the trick.

GARLIC IN MEDICINE

The number of ailments and afflictions that have been treated by applications of garlic over the years is almost endless: acne, alopecia, altitude sickness, animal bites, arteriosclerosis, asthma, athlete's foot, bee stings, bronchitis, bruises, cancer, catarrh, cold symptoms, constipation, eczema, epilepsy, exhaustion, flatulence, gangrene, graying hair, gastric disorders, headaches, hypertension, hypoglycaemia, insanity, jaundice, leprosy, most poisons, obesity, open wounds, piles, poison ivy, rabies, scabies, sciatica, scurvy, senility, snakebite, toothache, tuberculosis, whooping cough, and worms.

The ancient Egyptians, who were the first to practice medicine as we know it, featured many garlic-based cures in their pharmacopoeia. These were adapted by both Hippocrates (460–377 BC), known as the Father of Medicine, who recognized its value as a diuretic and a laxative, and by Dioscorides (40–90), whose medical texts were standard works until the late Middle Ages. The Chinese are believed to have used garlic medicinally since 2000 BC, while in India, the 5000-year-old system of Ayurvedic medicine, which features garlic-based cures for such ailments as heartburn, hoarseness, and typhus, still flourishes.

In the Middle Ages in Europe, books emerged, packed with plant-based recipes and lore, these books combined the folk medicine of the time (such as the tying of cut garlic cloves to the soles of the feet as a cough cure) and a growing interest in and appreciation of botany and natural science, and it was at this time that the fundamental principles of what we now know as homeopathy, naturopathy, and herbalism emerged. These disciplines remained popular until the end of the nineteenth century, by which time the medical mainstream had turned to the more "scientific" methods of a newly industrial society, but they are now enjoying a resurgence and winning new supporters.

(above) The chef with the flaming pan is cooking at the Gilroy Garlic Festival, an annual event held in Gilroy, California.

(left) In China, the shoots of garlic are eaten as often as the bulbs.

(right) Chinese men taking exercise before their morning meal which will contain herbs and garlic for health.

SOUPS & APPETIZERS

ARCADIAN GARLIC SOUP

SERVES 4 ~ 6

In "The Passionate Shepherd To His Love," the poet Virgil mentions "a fragrant soup of pounded garlic and wild-thyme for the reapers wearied by the scorching heat." This could be the sort of thing he had in mind.

INGREDIENTS

15–20 garlic cloves, unpeeled

5 Tbsp olive oil

5 cups chicken or veal stock

2 tsp fresh thyme

½ tsp salt

freshly ground white pepper

3 egg yolks

sliced French bread or toast, to serve

grated cheese, to serve

Blanch the garlic in boiling water for 1 minute, drain, and peel. Cook it, but do not let it brown, in half the oil for 10 minutes. Add the stock, thyme, salt, and plenty of white pepper. Simmer for 30 minutes and check the seasoning.

Sieve or blend the soup, keeping a few garlic cloves whole. Return the soup to its saucepan and keep hot.

Beat the egg yolks and gradually add the remaining oil. Stir a couple of spoonfuls of the soup in to the egg mixture, remove the soup from the heat, and add the egg in a thin stream, stirring well.

Serve immediately with sliced French bread or toast, and a sprinkling of grated cheese in each bowl.

GARLIC ONION SOUP

SERVES 6

INGREDIENTS

vegetable oil for frying

1 large onion, sliced

3 garlic bulbs, finely chopped

1 Tbsp all-purpose flour

½ tsp Dijon mustard

4½ cups vegetable stock

1 cup dry white wine

salt and freshly ground black pepper

a little butter

6 slices of French bread

6 slices Gruyère cheese, about 1 oz each

Heat the oil in a large saucepan. Add the onions and shortly after add the garlic. Keep on a low heat.

Stir in the flour, then add the Dijon mustard, stock, and wine, stirring the mixture continually.

Simmer until the onions are soft, then season to taste.

Butter the bread and top each with a slice of cheese.

Pour the soup into 6 individual ovenproof dishes. Float a slice of bread on each and place under a preheated broiler until the cheese is browned and bubbling. Serve immediately.

CREAM OF GARLIC AND MUSHROOM SOUP

SERVES 3 ~ 4

Add garlic to this classic recipe for a change.

INGREDIENTS

2 heads of garlic (about 25 cloves)

4 cups white button mushrooms, wiped and halved

6 Tbsp butter

1 tsp fresh thyme

4 Tbsp all-purpose flour

⅔ cup chicken stock

⅔ cup milk

⅓ cup light or cereal cream

salt and freshly ground black pepper

2 Tbsp chopped parsley, to serve

2 oz button mushrooms, thinly sliced, to serve

Separate the garlic cloves and blanch them in boiling water for 1 minute. Drain and peel.

Sweat the mushrooms in the butter for 5 minutes. Lift them out of the pan and keep to one side.

Add the garlic and thyme to the butter and mushroom juices and gently cook with the lid on for 10–15 minutes, until the garlic cloves are just tender.

Stir in the flour and cook for several minutes. Turn up the heat and add the stock and milk, a little at a time, stirring well. Simmer the mixture for 10 minutes.

Add the mushrooms and simmer for another minute until they are heated through. Remove from the heat and stir in the cream. Season with salt and pepper to taste.

Serve sprinkled with the chopped parsley and thinly sliced crisp, raw mushrooms, for texture.

STUFFED MUSHROOMS

SERVES 4

Garlic goes particularly well with mushrooms. Bring back this old favorite as a tasty start to a meal.

INGREDIENTS

8 large, flat mushrooms

6 Tbsp butter, softened

2–3 garlic cloves, finely chopped

2 Tbsp fresh white bread crumbs

1 Tbsp finely chopped parsley

Wipe the mushrooms and cut off the stems, as close as possible to the caps.

Mash together the butter and garlic.

Arrange the mushrooms, gill side up, on a greased baking sheet and dot with the garlic and butter mixture. Cover with foil and bake at 350°F for 15–20 minutes or until the mushrooms are just tender.

Remove the foil and top the mushrooms with the bread crumbs and parsley. Broil at a high heat until the bread crumbs are browned.

Stuffed Mushrooms ▶

GREEN "PISTOU" SOUP

SERVES 4

The lovely, all-green color is an unexpected delight. Add pasta if you like, and to make
a classic pistou add a handful of cooked vermicelli to the pot.

INGREDIENTS

1 leek, chopped

2 onions, chopped

5 garlic cloves, coarsely chopped

3 Tbsp extra-virgin olive oil

3 medium ripe, yellow tomatoes, diced

salt and freshly ground black pepper
to taste

1¾ pints vegetable stock

1¾ pints water

3 small zucchini, cut into bite-sized pieces

1 medium sized, waxy potato,
peeled and diced

¼ cabbage, thinly sliced

¾ cup fresh, white, shell beans (such as
coco, shelled and cooked,
or cooked cannellini)

8 chard or spinach leaves, thinly sliced

¼–½ bunch broccoli, cut into flowerets

handful of green beans,
cut into bite-sized pieces

1 batch of pistou (page 173), to serve

extra shredded Parmesan, to serve

Lightly sauté the leek, onion, and garlic in the olive oil until they are soft, then add the tomatoes and cook over a medium heat for about 10 minutes. Season to taste with salt and black pepper.

Add the vegetable stock and water, the zucchini, potato, and cabbage, and continue to cook over a medium heat until the potatoes are just tender and the zucchini are quite soft. The cabbage will be soft by now, too.

Add the white beans, chard or spinach leaves, broccoli, and green beans, and cook for about another 5 minutes, or until the broccoli and green beans are cooked through.

Serve immediately in bowls with a tablespoon or two of pistou stirred in, accompanied by shredded Parmesan to taste. Do not heat the pistou, or its fragrance will dissipate.

CREAMY PURÉE OF WHITE BEANS AND PORCINI

SERVES 4 ~ 6

Humble beans puréed with luxurious wild mushrooms create a classic soup through the southwest of France. The soup is sometimes served with a scattering of shredded prosciutto, a shaving of truffle, a drizzle of truffle oil, or a scattering of diced foie gras.

INGREDIENTS

2½ cups cooked white beans
(such as cannellini or lingots)

10 cups stock, preferably ham

⅓ cup diced ham or bacon (such as
pancetta or prosciutto)

1 carrot, diced

1 baking potato, diced

2–3 tsp fresh thyme leaves

5 garlic cloves, roughly chopped

2 oz dried mushrooms (such as porcini)

1 cup water

3 Tbsp brandy

salt and freshly ground black pepper

2 Tbsp sweet butter or
3 Tbsp heavy cream

In a saucepan, combine the beans with the stock, ham or bacon, carrot, potato, half the thyme, and the garlic. Bring to a boil, then reduce the heat to low, and simmer for about 30 minutes, until the vegetables are tender and cooked through.

Meanwhile, place the mushrooms with the water and brandy in a saucepan. Gradually bring to a boil, then reduce the heat, and simmer for about 15 minutes until the mushrooms are tender.

Remove the mushrooms from the liquid, chop roughly, and add them to the soup. Strain the liquid, discarding the gritty bits, and add the strained liquid to the soup.

Mix the soup in the blender or food processor until smooth. Taste for seasoning, then stir in the butter or cream. Serve immediately in warmed bowls, garnished with thyme.

CLASSIC GREEK VEGETABLE SOUP

SERVES 6 ~ 8

Serve this classic Greek soup with freshly baked olive bread (eliopitta).

INGREDIENTS

½ cup olive oil

2 garlic cloves, crushed

2 onions, finely chopped

8 oz cabbage, finely shredded

3 carrots, chopped

3 celery sticks, chopped

2 large potatoes, peeled and diced

4 pints vegetable stock or water

4 tomatoes, skinned, seeded, and chopped

salt and freshly ground black pepper

4 Tbsp chopped fresh parsley

2 oz feta or kefalotyri cheese, shredded

Heat the olive oil in a large saucepan and add the garlic and onion. Cook for 5 minutes, until the onion is softened but not colored. Add the cabbage and continue to cook for another 3–4 minutes.

Add the carrots and celery to the saucepan, stir and cook for a further 5 minutes. Add the potatoes, stir and cook gently for another 5 minutes, until the vegetables are softened. Next pour in the vegetable stock or water and stir well. Increase the heat to bring the soup to a boil. Cover and simmer for 12–15 minutes. Add the tomato and season to taste with salt and freshly ground black pepper.

Re-cover the pan and gently simmer the soup for about 1 hour. Stir in the parsley just before the end of the cooking time. Serve sprinkled with shredded cheese.

FRAGRANT LETTUCE SOUP

SERVES 4 ~ 6

INGREDIENTS

6 garlic cloves, unpeeled

2 large Romaine lettuces

3 Tbsp finely chopped onion

3 Tbsp butter

4 Tbsp all-purpose flour

½ tsp sugar

salt and freshly ground black pepper

3¾ cups milks or milk and water, mixed

2 egg yolks

3 Tbsp light or cereal cream

I Tbsp chopped fresh parsley, chives, or
mint, to serve

Baked Garlic Croutons, to serve (page 61)

Plunge the unpeeled garlic cloves into boiling water and simmer for about 8 minutes. Drain, peel, and chop them coarsely.

Wash the lettuce and shred the leaves finely. Stew it gently with the onions in the butter for 5 minutes.

Stir in the parboiled garlic and cook for a further 5 minutes. Remove the vegetables from the heat and add the flour, sugar, and a little salt and pepper. Return to the heat and add the milk. Bring the mixture to a boil and simmer for 15 minutes, or until the vegetables are tender.

Either sieve or blend the soup and return it to the saucepan. Check the seasoning to taste.

Combine the egg yolks and cream, stir them into the soup, and heat to just below boiling point (if boiled, the egg yolks will get stringy).

To serve, sprinkle the chopped fresh parsley, chives, or mint over each bowlful and serve with Baked Garlic Croutons. For a more intense flavor, add a handful of roughly chopped watercress leaves to the stewing lettuce soup.

FLOATING ISLAND SOUP

SERVES 6

INGREDIENTS

8 oz fish trimmings

1 good-sized bunch of parsley

2–3 sprigs of fresh dill

5 cups water

1 medium onion, sliced

1¼ cups white wine, or wine
and water mixed

salt and freshly ground white pepper

3 cups/12 oz potatoes, peeled

1 small leek (white part only)

2 garlic cloves, unpeeled

½ Tbsp tomato paste

2 egg whites

1 Tbsp Parmesan cheese

1 tsp garlic juice

18 peeled shrimp, to serve

In a large saucepan, simmer the fish trimmings, parsley, dill, water, onion, and white wine with a little salt and pepper for 30 minutes.

Cut the potatoes into 1-inch chunks, and then cut the leeks into ½-inch slices.

Strain off the fish stock into a clean pan and add to it the potatoes, the leek, garlic, and the tomato paste. Simmer for 15–20 minutes, until the potato is cooked.

Either sieve or blend the soup until smooth. Return to the saucepan and season with salt and pepper to taste. Bring slowly to a boil.

Whip the egg whites with a good pinch of salt until they are really stiff. Fold in the Parmesan cheese, garlic juice, and a little white pepper.

Drop tablespoonfuls of the egg white mixture into the simmering soup and poach for about 5 minutes or until firm.

Serve immediately using 3 of the shrimp for each bowl.

COOK'S TIP

For a simpler soup, omit the egg white mixture and stir 1 tablespoon of light or cereal cream into each bowlful of soup. Serve with Baked Garlic Croutons (page 61).

CHICKEN SOUP WITH AVOCADO, GARBANZO BEANS, AND CHIPOTLES

SERVES 4 ~ 6

The soup is said to have originated in the Mexico City suburb of Tlapan, where food vendors try to capture the appetite of the strolling diners. One soup-seller hit upon the simple combination we think of today as Tlapan: avocado, chipotle, garbanzo beans, chicken stock, and lime.

INGREDIENTS

3 garlic cloves, coarsely chopped

I Tbsp olive oil

2 zucchini, cut into bite-sized pieces

½ carrot, thinly sliced

4¼ cups chicken stock

2 cups cooked, drained garbanzo beans

1–2 canned chipotle chiles, cut into strips, plus a little of the marinade

2 green onions, thinly sliced

about I cup shredded chicken

I avocado, peeled, pitted, and diced

I Tbsp chopped fresh cilantro

handful of tortilla chips, preferably low-salt ones

I lime, cut into wedges

Warm the garlic in the olive oil without browning. Add the zucchini, carrot, chicken stock, and garbanzo beans, then bring to a boil. Reduce the heat and simmer for about 10 minutes or until the vegetables are tender.

Ladle the soup into bowls and garnish each with a little chipotle, green onions, shredded chicken, avocado, cilantro, tortilla chips, and wedges of lime.

COOK'S TIP

Simmer cooked drained hominy in place of the garbanzo beans. The earthy, bland hominy is sensational with the smoky hot chipotle, creamy avocado, and sharp tangy lime.

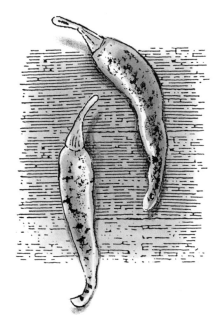

BEEF, EGGPLANT, AND BELL PEPPER SOUP

SERVES 4 ~ 6

A spicy broth or soup with the flavors of the Pacific Rim. Serve this as a lunch or supper dish with bread, or add a spoonful of cooked rice to each helping to make more substantial a dish.

INGREDIENTS

4 oz boneless chuck steak

3 Tbsp peanut oil

1 large onion, finely chopped

4 garlic cloves, finely chopped

1 small eggplant, finely diced

1 hot red chile, seeded and very finely chopped

1 green bell pepper, cored, deseeded, and finely sliced

1–inch piece fresh ginger, peeled, and finely sliced

1 stick lemon grass, bruised and finely chopped

3 fresh lime leaves, finely shredded (use dried if fresh are not available)

5 cups well-flavored broth

soy sauce, to taste

salt, to taste

Cut the beef into ½-inch strips, then slice it very finely. Heat the oil in a large pan, add the beef, and cook quickly until well browned. Add the onion, garlic, eggplant, chile, bell pepper, ginger, and lemon grass, then cover the pan and cook slowly for 4–5 minutes.

Add the lime leaves and broth, then bring to a boil. Cover and simmer for at least 1 hour, until all the ingredients are tender and the flavors have blended together.

Season the soup to taste with soy sauce and salt. Serve with crusty bread or rice if you wish.

COUNTRYSIDE SOUP OF MUSHROOMS AND FRENCH LENTILS

SERVES 4 ~ 6

Serve a bowlful of this soup on a cold winter's day accompanied by crusty whole-wheat bread and some sour cream to spoon into the soup.

INGREDIENTS

½ cup French lentils

3 bay leaves

3 cups water

3 cups stock

2–3 potatoes, peeled and diced

1 carrot, chopped

8–12 oz flat black mushrooms, diced

5 garlic cloves, chopped

3 Tbsp olive oil

salt and freshly ground
black pepper, to taste

1–2 tsp chopped fresh thyme or savory

Combine the French lentils with the bay leaves and water in a saucepan. Bring to a boil, reduce the heat to low, and cook, covered, until the lentils are just tender but not falling apart. Remove the bay leaves.

Add the stock, potatoes, and carrot, and cook over medium heat.

Meanwhile, sauté the mushrooms with the garlic in the olive oil. Season with salt and pepper. When the potatoes are cooked through and beginning to fall apart, add the sautéed mushrooms to the soup, along with the thyme or savory.

Continue to cook for 15–20 minutes more, crushing the potatoes as you stir. Taste, adjust the seasoning if necessary, and serve hot.

COOK'S TIP
The best and most flavorsome stock is always homemade. Fresh stock is now widely available in markets. Stock cubes may be used at a pinch, unless the recipe states otherwise.

BOUILLABAISSE

SERVES 8

*Variations on this substantial soup—almost a fish stew—abound all over the Mediterranean,
the only constant being to use as many different types of fish as you can.*

INGREDIENTS

2½ lb fish

8 oz shellfish

4 Tbsp olive oil

1 large onion, coarsely chopped

4 garlic cloves, crushed

2 cups white wine

1 Tbsp fresh mixed herbs

pinch of saffron threads (optional)

1 cup/12 oz tomatoes, skinned, seeded,
and coarsely chopped

1 tsp sugar

salt and freshly ground white pepper

a little cayenne

16 slices of French bread fried in oil or
Clarified Garlic Butter (page 180)

Clean the fish and cut it into equal-sized pieces. Small fish can be left whole. Scrub any mussels or clams, and beard the mussels. Shell any shrimp and, if using scallops, cut the meat out of the shell and halve.

Separate the fish onto two plates, one for firm-fleshed fish and one for soft-fleshed varieties. Keep any squid or inkfish separate.

Heat the oil in a large saucepan and fry the onion until it begins to brown. Add the garlic and cook for several minutes. Add the wine, mixed herbs, and saffron, if used.

Simmer for 5 minutes, add any squid or inkfish, and cook for 10 minutes. Add the firm-fleshed fish and cook for 10 more minutes. Add the soft-fleshed fish and simmer until almost cooked. You may need to add some water so that the liquid still covers the fish.

Add the tomatoes, prepared shellfish, and sugar, and season with salt, pepper, and a little cayenne. Cook for a further 5 minutes, by which time any clams or mussels will have opened up.

Serve with the fried bread and a good dollop of Aïoli (page 171) in each bowl.

BASQUE WILD MUSHROOM SOUP

SERVES 4

The flavors of wild mushrooms and chorizo combine deliciously in this highly flavored and robust soup,
which is surprisingly light, and suitable for the summer or warm weather in the fall.

INGREDIENTS

1 oz mixed exotic mushrooms (such as trompette de la mort, mousserons, and morels), including a few slices of dried porcini or 1 oz porcini

2 cups water

1 onion, chopped

4 garlic cloves, roughly chopped

2 Tbsp olive oil

8 oz drained, cooked, garbanzo beans

2 cups chicken stock

¼–½ tsp chopped fresh rosemary

2–3 oz Spanish chorizo, cut into julienne strips

salt and freshly ground black pepper, to taste

Place the mushrooms in a large saucepan with the water, and bring to a boil. Remove from the heat and leave to rehydrate for about 15 minutes. Squeeze out the mushrooms, letting all of the liquid drip back into the pan.

Chop the mushrooms, strain the liquid, and set both aside.

Lightly sauté the onion and garlic in the olive oil. Add the garbanzo beans and cook for a few moments more, then add the strained mushroom liquid, and bring to a boil.

Take about a quarter of the garbanzo bean mixture and mix in a blender or food processor until it is smooth. Add a little more liquid from the saucepan if necessary. Return the mixture to the saucepan, along with the mushrooms, stock, rosemary, and chorizo. Bring to a boil, reduce the heat, and simmer for à few minutes until warmed through.

Taste for seasoning, and add more salt and pepper if necessary. Serve the soup immediately.

COOK'S TIP
For a quick soup, use canned rather than dried garbanzo beans. The result will be just as good.

GANOUG GANOUG

SERVES 4

INGREDIENTS

2 eggplants

2–3 garlic cloves, finely crushed

2 Tbsp olive oil

1 Tbsp lemon juice

salt and freshly ground black pepper

Wrap the eggplants in oiled kitchen foil, place on a baking sheet, and bake for 30–45 minutes or until soft.

Split open the eggplant and scoop out the pulp. Mash the pulp with the garlic, oil, and lemon juice. Season with salt and pepper to taste, and chill.

Serve very cold with warm, dry toast and chilled fresh butter.

TOMATO AND GREEN BELL PEPPER GAZPACHO

SERVES 4

The creaminess of this thick soup comes from the puréed stale bread and olive oil, which are blended with the vegetables. It is a specialty of Andalusia and is traditionally made by pounding, although a blender works just as well. Serve with a crisp garnish.

INGREDIENTS

4 oz stale country bread

¾ cup extra-virgin olive oil

1½ cups/12 oz ripe tomatoes, diced

1 green bell pepper, diced

4 garlic cloves, finely chopped

2 Tbsp sherry vinegar

salt, to taste

GARNISHES

1 hard-cooked egg, chopped

1 slice country bread, cut into cubes and browned in olive oil

1–2 slices Serrano or Parma ham, cut into thin strips

Cut or break the bread into bite-sized pieces. Place them in the food processor or blender, pour over cold water to cover and leave for a moment or two. Drain.

Add the olive oil, tomatoes, bell pepper, garlic, sherry vinegar, and salt. Blend until a thick purée forms. Season to taste and chill until ready to serve with the optional garnishes.

EGGPLANT GUACAMOLE

SERVES 4 ~ 6

For all diet-conscious lovers of Mexican food! This is a low-calorie version of the traditional avocado dip.

INGREDIENTS

1 large eggplant

1 avocado, peeled and finely chopped

grated zest and juice of 1 lime

2 tomatoes, seeded and finely chopped

1 green chile, seeded and
very finely chopped

1 Tbsp very finely chopped onion

1–2 garlic cloves, crushed

salt and freshly ground black pepper

olive oil, to drizzle

paprika, to sprinkle

Preheat the oven to 425°F. Prick the eggplant all over, then place it on a baking sheet and roast for 30–40 minutes, until wrinkled and tender. Cover with a damp cloth and leave to cool completely,

Peel the eggplant, then chop the flesh into small pieces. Blend to a fairly smooth paste in a blender or food processor, then turn into a small bowl.

Toss the avocado in the lime juice, then add to the eggplant with the remaining ingredients. Stir the mixture carefully until well combined. Season generously with salt and pepper, then drizzle with a little olive oil and sprinkle with paprika.

Serve the guacamole with tortilla chips or warm toast.

ROASTED TOMATOES WITH OLIVE OIL, GARLIC, AND BASIL

SERVES 4

Serve with crusty bread to soak up the juices and tomato. Capers, olives, or anchovies can be scattered on top, for a salty Mediterranean flavor.

INGREDIENTS

12 small to medium sized ripe, flavorful tomatoes

4–5 Tbsp extra-virgin olive oil

½–1 tsp balsamic vinegar, or to taste

coarse sea salt, to taste

3–5 garlic cloves, finely chopped

handful of fresh basil, coarsely torn

Arrange the tomatoes in a casserole, about an inch or so apart, and drizzle lightly with a little of the olive oil (1–2 teaspoons).

Preheat the oven to 425°F. Place the tomatoes in the oven and roast for 20 minutes, then reduce the heat to 325°F and cook for a further 30 minutes. The tomato skins should be darkened and cracked, to the point of peeling off. Remove from the oven and allow to cool, preferably overnight when the juices will thicken.

Remove the skins of the tomatoes and squeeze them, letting the juices run back onto the tomatoes.

Serve at room temperature, drizzled with olive oil, balsamic vinegar, and sprinkled with salt, garlic, and basil.

SNAIL BUNS

SERVES 4

For many people, the high point of the snail-eating experience is mopping up the aromatic juices with fresh bread. Served this way, the juices are absorbed by the bread during cooking, which is then eaten as a bonne bouche. *The bun tops can be used for dipping.*

INGREDIENTS

4 large soft white rolls

3–4 garlic cloves, crushed

½ cup/4 oz butter, softened

1 Tbsp chopped scallions (green part only)

1 Tbsp chopped parsley

salt and freshly ground black pepper

16 canned snails with shells

Cut the top third off each roll and scoop out four depressions, each large enough to hold a snail shell.

Mash the garlic with the softened butter, scallions, and parsley, and season with a little salt and pepper.

Drain the snails and put each into its shell. Fill the shells with the garlic and butter mixture.

Put 4 stuffed snail shells into each bun, keeping them as upright as possible. Arrange them on a baking sheet and cook at 425°F for about 7 minutes or until the butter has melted and the snails are heated through.

Cover the filled buns with their tops, warm through to serve.

TARAMASALATA

SERVES 4

The only thing this delicate creation has in common with the salty, pink, commercially produced taramasalata is the name. This version is only worth making if you can get fresh *smoked cod roe, dark red and veined on the outside and reddish-pink inside. Cod roe in cans or jars is always very salty.*

INGREDIENTS

2 oz slice of crustless white bread

1 cup/8 oz fresh smoked cod roe

2 garlic cloves, crushed

6 Tbsp olive oil

lemon juice to taste

1 lemon cut into wedges, to serve

pita bread, to serve

Soak the bread in water and squeeze it out.
Skin the roe and mash it together with the bread and garlic.

Gradually stir in the olive oil, adding lemon juice to taste.

Serve with lemon wedges and Greek pita bread, or as a topping for baked potatoes.

COOK'S TIP

Taramasalata can also be made in a blender, although the texture will be much lighter and thicker, and you will need to thin the mixture with a little light or cereal cream or extra lemon juice.

TARTE MARIE-ODILE

SERVES 4 ~ 6

Slice this tart into thin wedges and serve on its own as an appetizer.

INGREDIENTS

1½ cups all-purpose flour

pinch of salt

1 tsp paprika

2 pinches of cayenne

½ cup/4 oz butter, softened

1 Tbsp Parmesan cheese

1 egg yolk

3 cups Ratatouille (page 145), leaving
out the basil and feta

3 Tbsp sour cream

1 Tbsp coarsely chopped parsley

Sieve together the flour, salt, paprika, and cayenne. Blend in the softened butter until the mixture resembles fine bread crumbs.

Add the Parmesan and egg yolk and, if the pastry seems too stiff and crumbly, add a little cold water.

Press the pastry into a shallow cake pan or a 9-inch pie plate. Cover with foil and baking beans and bake at 400°F for about 20 minutes. Remove the foil and return the pastry to the oven for a further 5 minutes to brown. While still warm, remove the pastry shell from its pan and put it on a wire rack to cool. Place the pastry shell on a pretty plate and fill with the chilled, drained Ratatouille. Pour over the cream in a spiral, and sprinkle with the parsley.

Serve immediately or the pastry will lose its crispness.

GARLIC CHEESECAKE TART

SERVES 6

INGREDIENTS

8 oz shortcrust pastry

1 head garlic (about 12 cloves)

handful of parsley

handful of watercress or spinach

¾ cup cream cheese

½ cup light or cereal cream

3 eggs, beaten

salt and freshly ground black pepper

Preheat the oven to 425°F. Line an 8-inch flan dish with the pastry and cover with foil. Fill with baking beans and bake blind for 10–15 minutes until firm. Remove the baking beans and foil and leave the pastry shell to cool.

Simmer the unpeeled garlic cloves for 25 minutes until soft. Drain and, when cool, mash to a paste.

Cook the parsley and watercress or spinach in a pan of boiling water for 7–10 minutes until tender. Drain and refresh under cold water. Squeeze out the excess liquid, and chop finely. Mix with the garlic paste, seasoning with a little salt and pepper to taste. Spread the mixture over the bottom of the cooked pastry shell.

Mash the cream cheese with the cream and a little salt and pepper until smooth. Add the beaten eggs. Pour over the garlic paste and bake at 350°F for about 25 minutes until just set. Serve warm.

◄ *Tarte Marie-Odile*

CRAB-STUFFED MUSHROOMS

SERVES 6 ~ 8

These mushrooms are very rich and very delicious. Even people who usually think they do not like seafood will love this stuffing.

INGREDIENTS

24 large, flat mushrooms

2 Tbsp butter

4 green onions, chopped

I garlic clove, minced

½ tsp salt

½ tsp cayenne

¼ cup dry bread crumbs

¼ cup heavy cream or half-and-half

12 oz fresh crab meat, picked over, or frozen or canned, well drained

Parmesan cheese

Clean the mushrooms and separate the stems from the caps. Meanwhile, finely chop the stems. Steam the mushrooms for 5 minutes, then set aside.

In a skillet over medium heat, melt the butter. Add the chopped stems, green onions, and garlic and cook for 8–10 minutes or until most of the liquid has evaporated. Add the salt, cayenne, bread crumbs, and cream, and mix well. Gently stir in the crab meat and cook until just heated through.

Stuff the mushroom caps with the crab mixture, mounding a little on each top. Sprinkle with Parmesan cheese. Arrange on a lightly greased baking sheet. Bake at 350°F for 10 minutes, then broil for 2–3 minutes until the cheese turns golden brown.

SHERBET TOMATOES

SERVES 4

INGREDIENTS

2 large beefsteak tomatoes

salt

2 garlic cloves, crushed

freshly ground black pepper

generous handful of fresh mint leaves

juice of I large lemon

2 tsp sugar

2 egg whites

sprigs of mint, to serve

Halve the tomatoes horizontally. Scoop out and reserve the seeds and cores.

Sprinkle the insides of the tomato shells with a little salt and turn them upside down to drain. Smear the inside of each tomato shell with the crushed garlic and sprinkle with plenty of pepper.

Press the tomato seeds and cores through a sieve to extract the juice, and make up to ⅔ cup with water.

Combine the mint leaves, tomato juice, lemon juice, and sugar in a blender. The mixture should not be too smooth.

Pack into an ice-cube tray and freeze for about an hour, until crystalline but still slightly mushy.

Whip the egg whites with a couple of pinches of salt until it forms soft peaks, and fold it into the semi-frozen mint mixture. Freeze until firm, stirring occasionally.

Pile the sherbet into each tomato half and garnish with a sprig of mint.

PAPAYA CRAB

SERVES 4

According to Jamaican folklore, a goat tied to a papaya tree won't be there in the morning.
This luxurious combination of papaya and crabmeat will disappear a lot quicker.

INGREDIENTS

2 ripe papayas, each 10–12 oz

¼ cup whipped cream

½ cup mayonnaise

Garlic Dressing (page 180) or garlic juice to taste

lime or lemon juice

freshly ground white pepper

12 oz crabmeat

Split the papayas and remove the seeds and "strings." Mix the whipped cream with the mayonnaise. Homemade mayonnaise is much richer than commercial brands, so you may need to add a little more whipped cream to lighten it.

Flavor to taste with garlic dressing or garlic juice, lime or lemon juice, and a little white pepper. This dressing should be delicate.

Combine the dressing with the crabmeat and pile into the papaya halves. Serve chilled.

COOK'S TIP

For Melon Crab, use two small melons, halved and deseeded, instead of the papayas. The fragrant, orange- or peach-fleshed varieties of melon, such as Charentais and Canteloup, are particularly good for this.

SHRIMP PANCAKES

SERVES 4 ~ 6

INGREDIENTS

1½ lb cooked shrimp in their shells

juice of ½ lemon

1 small onion, quartered

2 garlic cloves, coarsely chopped

1¼ cups dry white wine

½ tsp dill

½ a bayleaf

3–4 parsley stalks

sprig of thyme

1¼ cups all-purpose flour

2 eggs, beaten

½ cup/3½ oz butter

1¼ cups milk

½ cup light or cereal cream

salt and freshly ground white pepper

Wash and peel the shrimp. Cover the shrimp meat and put it into the refrigerator. Simmer half the shells, the lemon juice, onion, garlic, wine, and herbs in a large saucepan for 30 minutes.

Make the pancake batter by sifting 1 cup of the flour with a good pinch of salt. Stir in the eggs. Then melt 2 tablespoons of the butter and add to the flour together with enough milk to make a fairly thick batter. Leave the batter to stand in the refrigerator for at least 1 hour.

Strain the shrimp shell stock and reduce, if necessary, to about ⅔ cup.

Melt 2 tablespoons of butter and add the remaining flour. Stir over a

moderate heat, without browning, for a couple of minutes. Add the stock and simmer for a further 5 minutes.

Remove from heat and add the shrimp and cream. Adjust the seasoning and keep warm.

To cook the pancakes, stir the chilled batter well (you may need to add a little more milk at this stage). Fry 1 tablespoonful at a time in a buttered pan, keeping each pancake warm as it is cooked. When all the

pancakes have been cooked, fill them with the shrimp mixture and arrange in a buttered baking dish. Dot with the remaining butter and brown under a moderate broiler for 5 minutes to heat through. Serve immediately.

GRIDDLED EGGPLANT AND GOAT'S CHEESE SALAD

SERVES 4

In this marinated salad, the spiced eggplant slices are broiled and served hot with goat's cheese. Do try a true goat's cheese, it is so good. The real thing should be eaten at its freshest.

INGREDIENTS

I eggplant, thinly sliced

olive oil, for frying

3½ oz soft goat's cheese, sliced

MARINADE

1½ tsp cumin seeds

½ tsp coarse sea salt

½ cup red wine

2 Tbsp olive oil

I Tbsp red wine vinegar

salt and freshly ground black pepper

I garlic clove, crushed

I Tbsp chopped fresh mint

I tsp sugar

Make the marinade. Heat a small skillet, then add the cumin seeds and dry fry them for 30–45 seconds, until fragrant and starting to brown. Turn the seeds into a mortar with the sea salt and pound them with a pestle until finely ground. Alternatively, crush with the end of a rolling pin.

Transfer the spice mixture to a shallow dish and add the remaining marinade ingredients. Add the eggplant slices, turning to coat we for at least 30 minutes.

Shake the eggplant slices dry, and reserve the marinade. Griddle the slices with a little oil in a griddle pan or skillet. Place in an ovenproof dish and top with the sliced cheese.

Drizzle with the remaining marinade then broil under moderate heat until lightly browned. Serve with crusty bread and a juicy tomato salad.

ROASTED BELL PEPPERS IN OIL

SERVES 4

Roasted bell peppers in olive oil are quintessential Mediterranean fare, eaten in a variety of guises throughout the Mediterranean and Middle East, but they are also the national dish of Romania, eaten with slabs of white brynza cheese (similar to feta) or with garlicky, broiled meatballs.

INGREDIENTS

3 each: red, yellow, and green bell peppers
(or 8–9 of any one kind)

1 Tbsp salt

½ cup wine vinegar

½ cup water

½ cup extra-virgin olive oil

5 garlic cloves, chopped

2 tsp paprika

½ tsp sugar, or to taste

sprig of thyme, to serve

2–3 oz diced brynza or
feta cheese, to serve

handful of black olives, to serve

Roast the bell peppers by placing them directly on the top of the stove and letting them cook just slightly away from the heat, until they are lightly and evenly charred. Alternatively, you can place the peppers on a baking sheet and broil them for about 15 minutes on each side, turning so that they brown in spots in an even manner.

Wrap them in a clean dish cloth or place them in a bowl or pan with a tight-fitting lid or in a plastic or paper bag, and seal tightly. Leave for about an hour until cool.

Remove the skin, using a paring knife. Run them under cold water carefully to get rid of excess bits of charred black skin, but not for long, as they may lose their smoky flavor too. When the peppers are peeled, use a paring knife to cut off the stem end, and remove both it and the seeds. Save any juices inside.

Cut the peppers into halves lengthwise, and combine them with their roasting juices, the salt, vinegar, water, olive oil, garlic, paprika, and sugar, as desired. Leave to chill for at least 2 hours, or overnight if possible.

Serve at room temperature as an antipasto, garnished with thyme. Sprinkle over the diced cheese and arrange the black olives on the platter.

CHEESE AND GUACAMOLE PIZZA WEDGES

MAKES 24 APPETIZER WEDGES

Tortillas baked with cheese are popular pizzas in the Southwest. Mexican restaurants in Arizona serve them on giant tortillas, 12 or more inches in diameter, but unless you make your own, that size is not readily available. This recipe uses 8-inch tortillas, which are easy to find, and are a good size for appetizers.

INGREDIENTS

1 ripe avocado

1 large garlic clove, chopped

2 Tbsp bottled pickled jalapeño pepper, chopped

2 tsp juice from pickled jalapeños

½ tsp salt

6 flour tortillas (8-inch diameter)

¾ cup bottled salsa

1½ cups shredded Cheddar cheese

To make the guacamole, mash the avocado with a fork. Add the chopped (or pressed) garlic and the chopped bottled jalapeño peppers, along with 2 teaspoons liquid from the bottle. Stir in the salt. Store in the refrigerator until ready to serve.

To make the pizzas, lightly toast the tortillas (easiest in a toaster oven). Remove from the oven and top each tortilla with 2 tablespoons of salsa, then ¼ cup of the shredded Cheddar cheese. Broil for about 3 minutes, until the cheese melts.

To serve, cut each tortilla into quarters. Top each quarter with a teaspoon of guacamole.

RIPE TOMATO AND BASIL BRUSCHETTA

SERVES 4

This delicious, oily, garlicky treat is on the menu all over northern Italy. It is one of the best things to eat in the summer, when you have good bread, good tomatoes, and good oil.

INGREDIENTS

4 thick slices of Italian country bread
(or French bread, if not available)

½ cup olive oil (or more, as needed)

6 very ripe, flavorful tomatoes, diced

handful of fresh, sweet basil leaves, torn

4 garlic cloves, chopped

coarse sea salt, to taste

Brush the bread with several tablespoons of the olive oil, then toast it on a baking sheet at 425°F for about 15 minutes, turning once or twice, or until crisp and golden brown.

Combine the tomatoes with the rest of the olive oil, basil, and garlic, sprinkle with coarse sea salt, and serve on the bread.

LEMON CHICKEN BROTH WITH HERB DUMPLINGS

SERVES 6

This delicate broth with herb-and-garlic-scented dumplings was inspired by avgolemono, *the classic Greek lemon and chicken soup.*

INGREDIENTS

2 cups soft white bread crumbs

1 garlic clove, crushed

1 Tbsp parsley, finely chopped

1 tsp dill, finely chopped

1 tsp mixed fresh herbs

salt and freshly ground black pepper

1 egg, beaten

a little seasoned all-purpose flour

5 cups well-flavored chicken stock

juice of 2 large lemons

6 sprigs of fresh dill, to serve

6 slices of lemon, to serve

Make the dumplings. Mix together the bread crumbs, garlic, parsley, dill, and mixed herbs. Season with a little salt and black pepper, and add enough of the beaten egg to form a soft dough.

Shape the mixture into small balls, about the size of a large marble, and roll each in the seasoned flour.

Bring the stock to a boil in a large saucepan and poach the dumplings for 5–8 minutes.

Remove from the heat, add the lemon juice, and adjust the seasoning.

Just before serving, add a sprig of dill and a slice of lemon to each bowl.

SNACKS & SAVORIES

FRIED GARLIC HALOUMI

MAKES ABOUT 16

INGREDIENTS

1¼ cups haloumi cheese
(available from most Greek delicatessens)

3–4 garlic cloves, crushed

1 Tbsp fresh mixed herbs, bruised and
torn into small pieces

1¼ cups olive oil

COOK'S TIP

Strained, the left-over oil is marvelous
for salad dressings and marinades.

Cut the cheese into 1-inch cubes and pack them into a shallow soufflé dish in a single layer. Sprinkle over the crushed garlic and herbs, and pour over the olive oil to cover the cheese cubes.

Cover the dish with a plate and leave in a cool place for at least 12 hours so that the flavors of the garlic and herbs permeate the cheese.

To cook the haloumi, drain off the garlic oil and fry the cheese for about 6 minutes in a few tablespoonfuls of the oil until golden all over.

Serve immediately with toothpicks. To serve as a first course, cut the haloumi into ¼-inch slices, marinate, fry, and serve with a sharp gooseberry sauce.

PIPERADE

SERVES 3 ~ 4

This makes a tasty brunch and is filling enough to keep you going until dinner time.

INGREDIENTS

2 Tbsp butter

1 medium onion, thinly sliced

1–2 garlic cloves, crushed

1 red bell pepper, seeded and thinly sliced

2 large tomatoes, skinned, seeded,
and coarsely chopped

4 eggs

salt and freshly ground black pepper

slice of hot buttered toast per
person, to serve

1 Tbsp parsley, chopped, to garnish

Melt the butter in a heavy saucepan, and cook the onions, garlic, and bell pepper for 15 minutes. Add the tomato and cook for a further 5 minutes.

Beat the eggs together with a little salt and pepper and pour this mixture over the vegetables.

Reduce down the heat and stir the mixture until the eggs are thick and the texture is creamy. Be careful not to overcook them.

Spread the mixture on hot, buttered toast and serve, sprinkled with parsley.

COOK'S TIP

For a more substantial version, add 1 cup of cubed, cooked ham with the tomatoes.

Piperade ▶

GARLIC BUTTERED NUTS

INGREDIENTS

1½ cups shelled almonds, cashews, or peanuts, or a mixture

2 Tbsp butter

1 Tbsp oil

2–3 garlic cloves, finely crushed

rock salt

Loosen and remove the almond skins by pouring boiling water over them and refreshing in cold water. Rub the brown skins off the peanuts and discard.

Melt the butter and oil with the garlic in a heavy frying pan and toss the nuts in it over a moderate heat for 3–5 minutes or until they are crisp and golden on the outside.

Drain on kitchen paper towels and sprinkle with rock salt. Serve warm.

COOK'S TIP
To make Devilled Garlic Nuts, add a little cayenne to the rock salt.

OMELET WITH MOUSSERONS

SERVES 4

This omelet from southwestern France has a real flavor of the fall. Use any mushrooms, especially porcini, or a mixture of common cultivated brown mushrooms with a few delicious dried mushrooms.

INGREDIENTS

12 oz mousserons, diced

1 slice (about 2 oz) prosciutto (or other strong-flavored raw ham), diced

3 garlic cloves, chopped

1–2 Tbsp chopped fresh parsley

2–3 Tbsp olive oil or butter

salt and freshly ground black pepper

8–10 eggs, lightly beaten

2–4 Tbsp milk

Lightly sauté the mushrooms together with the ham, garlic, and parsley, in about half the olive oil or butter, until just tender. Season to taste with salt and pepper, and set aside.

Combine the eggs with the milk.

Heat a small omelet pan if you are going to make 4 individual omelets or a large pan for a single large omelet or for 2 medium sized omelets. For 4 individual omelets, add 1–2 teaspoons of olive oil or butter to the hot pan, then pour in a quarter of the egg mixture. Cook for a few moments, then spoon in a quarter of the mushroom mixture. Roll the sides over and roll the omelet out of the pan. Repeat with the remaining ingredients.

To make a single large omelet, do the same, using all the egg and filling in one go. For 2 medium-size omelets, do the same but with half the mixture in each. Serve immediately.

Garlic Buttered Nuts ▶

TOMATO-CHILE EGGS

SERVES 4

In the Yucatán this classic dish would come sandwiched between two crisp tortillas, but with tortillas at the bottom only, the dish is more visually appealing.

INGREDIENTS

1¾ cups fresh or
canned tomatoes, chopped

1 onion, chopped

3 garlic cloves, minced

1–2 fresh chiles, chopped

salt and freshly ground black pepper

large dash of ground cumin

3 Tbsp olive oil

1 plantain, peeled and diced

1 Tbsp butter

4 tostadas

pickled pinto beans, seasoned with cumin

4 or 8 poached or fried eggs, kept warm

1 red bell pepper or 1 fresh large red
mild chile, roasted, deseeded, stemmed,
and peeled, then cut into strips

3–4 Tbsp cooked green peas, warm

3 Tbsp diced smoked ham

2 Tbsp chopped fresh cilantro

¾ cup flavorful white cheese
(such as feta) or mild white cheese
(such as Monterey Jack), diced

In a blender or food processor, purée the tomatoes with the onion, garlic, chiles, salt and pepper, and cumin.

Heat the oil in a skillet, then ladle in a little of the sauce and cook until the sauce reduces in volume and becomes almost paste-like. Ladle in some more sauce and repeat. Finally, pour in the remaining sauce, and simmer together for 5–10 minutes. Keep warm.

Lightly brown the plantain in butter. Set aside and keep warm.

Spread the tostadas with warm pickled beans, then top each with 1 or 2 poached or fried eggs.

Spoon the warm tomato sauce around or over the egg, then sprinkle with the diced plantain, roasted peppers or chiles, peas, ham, cilantro, and cheese.

JAZZED CECILS

SERVES 4 ~ 6

I lb ground beef
I small onion, grated
I cup fresh white bread crumbs
2–3 garlic cloves, crushed
2 tsp tomato paste
I tsp sugar
I tsp paprika
2 dashes of Tabasco sauce
I Tbsp mixed fresh herbs
I egg, beaten
salt and freshly ground black pepper
½ cup seasoned all-purpose flour
4 Tbsp butter
2 Tbsp oil
I cup thick unsweetened yogurt
I Tbsp chopped chives
I Tbsp chopped parsley

Combine the ground beef, onion, bread crumbs, garlic, tomato paste, sugar, paprika, Tabasco sauce, herbs, and egg. Season with salt and pepper.

Mold the mixture into small balls, about the size of a large marble, and roll these in the seasoned flour.

Fry the balls in the butter and oil for 5–10 minutes. Drain on absorbent kitchen paper and keep warm.

Make the dip. Mix together the yogurt, chives, and parsley and season with salt and pepper.

Serve the cecils with toothpicks with the yogurt dip in a separate dish.

ROLLED OMELET WITH GOAT'S CHEESE FILLING

SERVES 4

The goat's cheese filling is tangy and fresh, and the eggs are delicate when gently cooked in the fragrant olive oil.

INGREDIENTS

8 eggs, lightly beaten

2–3 Tbsp milk

salt and freshly ground white pepper

4–5 Tbsp extra-virgin olive oil

½ or more green chile, finely chopped

2 garlic cloves, finely chopped

4–6 oz goat's cheese

3 Tbsp chopped dill

3 Tbsp chopped fresh cilantro

sour cream to taste (optional)

Prepare 4 individual omelets, using 2 eggs for each, mixed with a little milk. Pour 1–2 tablespoons of olive oil into the omelet pan, and warm but don't overheat—it should smell fragrant and be almost smoking, but not quite.

Pour in the required amount of beaten egg, and cook for a few moments over a low heat, lifting the edges from the sides and letting the runny egg flow under. When the egg is nearly set, sprinkle in a quarter of the chile, garlic, goat's cheese, dill, and cilantro, and fold over.

Roll out of the pan and serve hot, with each omelet topped with a scoop of sour cream, if wished.

GARLIC TAPENADE

SERVES 6

On small pieces of toast, this snack can serve as a canapé.

INGREDIENTS

1 cup black olives

2–3 garlic cloves, coarsely chopped

⅓ cup canned anchovies

1 Tbsp capers

½ cup olive oil

medium French loaf, thinly sliced

Pit and coarsely chop the olives and blend them with the garlic, anchovies, and capers. Add the olive oil gradually.

Toast the bread on one side. Spread the untoasted side thickly with the mixture, and cook under a hot broiler until the edges are well browned. Serve warm.

This tapenade can also be served on fingers of crisp, buttered toast.

Rolled Omelet with Goat's Cheese Filling ▶

EGGPLANT AND TOMATO GALETTE

SERVES 4

This is delicious as a supper dish, but it could easily be stretched to feed more as an appetizer. Although it takes some time to prepare, the work can all be done in advance so that the galette can be baked at the last moment.

INGREDIENTS

butter, for greasing

6 large eggs, beaten

¼ cup milk

salt and freshly ground black pepper

olive oil, for frying

1 large eggplant, sliced

4 tomatoes, sliced

1–2 garlic cloves, thinly sliced

4 oz Mozzarella, thinly sliced

SAUCE

⅔ cup sour cream

⅔ cup thick plain yogurt

2 Tbsp chopped chives

grated zest and juice of ½ lemon

Preheat the oven to 400°F, and butter a round gratin dish, the same diameter as your omelet pan. Beat the eggs with the milk and a little seasoning, then use the mixture to make 3 fairly thick omelets. Stack the finished omelets on absorbent paper towels until required. (If you wish, finish the top of each omelet under a hot broiler to save turning them over in the pan.)

Heat 2–3 tablespoons of olive oil in a skillet. Add the eggplant and cook until just tender and lightly browned, adding more oil as necessary. Place one omelet in the bottom of the buttered dish, then arrange half the eggplant slices in a layer on top.

Season lightly, then cover with half the sliced tomatoes and garlic. Season again and top with a third of the Mozzarella. Repeat the layers, finishing with an omelet topped with Mozzarella.

Bake in the preheated oven for 20–25 minutes, until the galette is piping hot and the Mozzarella has melted and is lightly browned.

Mix together all the ingredients for the sauce while the galette is baking. Serve the galette cut into quarters, with the sauce spooned over and around it.

MAMMY PATTIES

MAKES 25 ~ 30

A cocktail version of West Indian Patties.

INGREDIENTS

2 medium onions, finely chopped

1½ Tbsp oil

1½ tsp turmeric

1 tsp ground coriander

½ tsp ground cumin

½ tsp paprika

½ tsp garam masala

pinch of cayenne or chili powder

3 garlic cloves, crushed

1 cup grated carrot

½ tsp sugar

12 oz ground beef

1 cup cooked rice

salt and freshly ground black pepper

12 oz puff pastry

3 Tbsp milk

Preheat the oven to 425°F. Cook the onions in hot oil with all the spices, except for ½ teaspoonful of turmeric, for several minutes, stirring well during cooking.

Add the garlic, carrot, and sugar, and cook on a lower heat for a further 10 minutes or until the onion is transparent.

Add the beef and stir over a medium heat for about 7 minutes or until the meat has lost its pinkness.

Stir in the cooked rice and season to taste. Leave to cool.

Roll out the puff pastry thinly on a well-floured board. Stamp it into 3-inch rounds, using a glass or a special cookie cutter.

Form the trimmings into a ball, roll out again, and repeat. Stack the rounds sifting a little flour between each, and store in the refrigerator.

To fill the patties, pile a generous teaspoonful of the meat filling slightly to one side of the center of each pastry round. Brush all round the rim with a little water and fold over the pastry to form a semicircle. Press the wetted wedges together with a fork and prick the top.

Dissolve the remaining turmeric in a little hot water and the milk.

Space the filled patties on well-greased baking sheets, brush them with the turmeric milk, and bake until crisp and brown. Serve warm.

OAXACA EGGS

SERVES 4

Cooking eggs to make a flat omelet then cutting it into strips makes an intriguingly different egg dish.

INGREDIENTS

2 lb tomatoes

6 small to medium sized onions, peeled and halved

10 garlic cloves, whole and unpeeled

2–3 Anaheim or poblano chiles, roasted, peeled, and sliced

3 fresh green chiles (such as serranos), thinly sliced

⅓ cup oil

salt and freshly ground black pepper

dash of cumin

dash of dried oregano

dash of sugar

8 eggs, lightly beaten

2 Tbsp chopped fresh cilantro, to garnish

a little chopped fresh chile (optional), to garnish

In an ungreased, heavy saucepan, lightly char the tomatoes, turning once or twice. Allow to cool.

Cut up the tomatoes and place in a blender or food processor with their skins. Lightly char the onions and garlic. Cut up the onions and add to the blender or food processor, then squeeze the garlic cloves out of their skins and add with the chiles. Whirl until a smooth purée is formed.

Heat 2 tablespoons of oil in a skillet, then ladle in the sauce. Cook over high heat until it thickens and condenses.

Season to taste with salt and pepper, cumin, oregano, and sugar to balance the acid-sweetness. Set aside.

Make flat omelets, like thin pancakes, in the remaining oil, cooking about 2 eggs at a time and turning them over. Stack on a plate, and slice into noodle-like ribbons.

Heat the omelet strips in the sauce until warmed through, then garnish with cilantro and a little fresh chile.

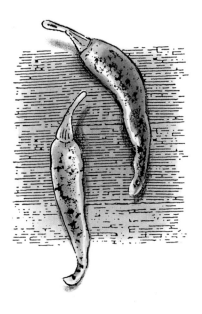

SCARBOROUGH EGGS

SERVES 2

This is the perfect dish for a light lunch. Serve it with plenty of crusty bread
and a green salad.

INGREDIENTS

3 Tbsp butter

1 garlic clove, crushed

½ Tbsp chopped parsley

½ tsp chopped fresh sage

2–3 blades of fresh rosemary, bruised

½ tsp fresh thyme

salt and freshly ground black pepper

4 fresh eggs

Melt the butter over a low heat and add the garlic, herbs, and seasoning. Cook gently for about 5 minutes until the garlic is transparent. Bring a small saucepan of water to a boil and cook the eggs for 3½–4 minutes. Shell them.

Add the eggs to the herb and garlic butter and turn them for a minute. Remove the rosemary blades and serve immediately.

BAKED EGGS WITH GREEN PEAS AND CREAM

SERVES 4

INGREDIENTS

2 cups/1 lb green peas, fresh
(shelled weight)

1 tsp sugar

sprigs of fresh mint

4 Tbsp butter

salt and freshly ground black pepper

8 eggs

1 garlic clove, finely crushed

⅔ cup light or cereal cream

Preheat the oven to 400°F. Boil the peas with the sugar and mint for 10–15 minutes or until just tender.

Drain, discarding the mint, and mash to a rough purée.

Stir in the butter, and season with salt and pepper to taste.

Divide the pea purée among 4 greased ramekin dishes and break 2 eggs over the top of each.

Mix the garlic into the cream and pour over eggs. Bake for 7–10 minutes, until the eggs are just set. Serve immediately.

COOK'S TIP

"Mushy peas" are a woefully neglected vegetable, and this is a delicious and unusual way of serving them. Warm the contents of a 15-ounce can, beat in a little butter, season with plenty of salt and pepper, and proceed as for the green pea purée.

GARLIC SCONES

MAKES 12

INGREDIENTS

2¼ cups all-purpose flour

2½ tsp baking powder

salt and freshly ground white pepper

4 Tbsp butter or margarine

2 garlic cloves, finely crushed

⅔ cup milk and water, mixed

Preheat the oven to 450°F. Then sieve the dry ingredients together and blend in the butter or margarine until the mixture resembles fine bread crumbs.

Add the crushed garlic and enough of the milk to form a soft, but not wet, dough. Divide the dough in two, dust with flour and press each half into a round about ¾ inch thick.

Put each round on a baking pan and divide into 6 sections with a knife, but do not separate the pieces.

Bake for 10–15 minutes until the scones are brown and well risen, and the underside sounds hollow when gently tapped.

Serve warm, split and buttered.

COOK'S TIP

Add ⅓ cup of coarsely chopped Cheddar cheese to the dough before adding the milk and water.

EGGS SCRAMBLED WITH TOMATOES, CHILES, AND TORTILLAS

SERVES 4

Scrambled with tomatoes, chiles, garlic, and spices, with a handful of crisp tortilla chips stirred in,
eggs make a marvelous supper or brunch dish.

INGREDIENTS

8–10 corn tortillas, cut into ½-inch strips
(or several large handfuls not too salty or
oily tortilla chips)

½ cup vegetable oil

6 garlic cloves, chopped

1 green bell pepper, diced

½ jalapeño or other green chile, thinly
sliced or chopped

3 Tbsp butter

1½ tsp ground cumin

5 ripe tomatoes, coarsely chopped

8 eggs, lightly beaten

3 Tbsp chopped fresh cilantro, to garnish

3–4 green onions, thinly sliced, to garnish

Fry the tortilla strips in the oil until they are golden but not dark brown. Remove them from the oil and drain on absorbent paper towels. (If you are using tortilla chips, simply break them up into bite-sized pieces.)

Fry the garlic, green bell pepper, and chile in a third of the butter for just 1 minute, then add the cumin and tomatoes and cook over medium heat for 3–4 minutes until the tomatoes are no longer runny. Remove from the pan and set aside.

Over a low heat, melt the remaining butter in a pan. Pour in the beaten eggs. Cook over a low heat, stirring, until the eggs begin to set.

Add the reserved chile-tomato mixture and tortilla strips and continue cooking, stirring once or twice, until the eggs are the consistency you wish. The tortilla strips should be pliable and chewy, neither crisp or soggy.

Serve immediately, topped with cilantro and green onions.

INDIVIDUAL PESTO PIZZAS

SERVES 4

Homemade pesto is so good it's worth growing a crop of basil in your garden in order to have easy access.
These pizzas make great appetizers, but are also good as the main course for lunch.

INGREDIENTS

4 pieces of pita bread (6-inch diameter)

1 small red onion, thinly sliced

1 small Roma tomato, thinly sliced

4 oz feta cheese, crumbled

PESTO SAUCE

½ cup fresh basil leaves
(soft stems and leaves only)

1 Tbsp pine nuts

1 large garlic clove, minced

4 Tbsp olive oil

2 oz fresh Parmesan cheese

First make the pesto sauce. Put the basil, pine nuts, garlic, olive oil, and Parmesan cheese in a blender or food processor and mix until thoroughly blended. Make ahead of time and refrigerate if you wish.

To make the pizza, toast the pita bread. Then top each piece with 1 tablespoon of pesto sauce, a slice of onion, a slice of tomato, and finally, an ounce of feta cheese. Lightly broil to warm through.

GARLIC ROULADE

SERVES 6

The spinach filling in this roulade gives it a colorful green pattern when you cut into it.
Serve with a tomato salad to add to the colorful display.

INGREDIENTS

6 Tbsp butter

4 Tbsp all-purpose flour

½ tsp English mustard

¼ tsp sugar

1¼ cups hot milk

2 Tbsp Parmesan cheese

2 oz Cheddar or Gruyère cheese, grated

2 garlic cloves, crushed

salt and freshly ground black pepper, to taste

4 eggs, separated

1½ lb fresh or ¾ lb frozen spinach

2 Tbsp light or cereal cream

Preheat the oven to 425°F. Melt 2 tablespoons of butter in a saucepan with the flour, mustard, and sugar, and stir for a couple of minutes, not letting it brown. Stir in the hot milk, a little at a time, and simmer for 5 minutes.

Add the cheese, crushed garlic, and salt and pepper. Remove from the heat, stir in 3 egg yolks, one at a time, and keep warm.

Boil the fresh spinach in lots of salted water for 5 minutes, until almost tender. Drain and refresh in cold water. Press out as much liquid as possible and chop finely. Turn into a pan with the remaining butter and a little seasoning, and cook gently for about 15 minutes to absorb all the butter. Check the seasoning and keep the mixture warm.

If you are using frozen spinach, cut the block into small pieces, using a freezer knife. Melt the butter, add the spinach pieces and cook very gently until thawed, turn up the heat a little, cook for a further 5 minutes, season to taste and keep warm.

Whip the egg whites with a pinch of salt until stiff. Beat a spoonful of egg white into the cheese sauce to loosen it up.

Carefully fold the cheese sauce into the remaining egg white and pour the mixture into a well-greased, foil-lined jelly roll pan. Bake for 5–7 minutes, until just set.

Tip out immediately on to a dish cloth rung out in hot water. Spread with three-quarters of the hot spinach purée, into which you have beaten the remaining egg yolk. Roll up as you would a jelly roll—it helps if you gradually pull up one end of the dish cloth as you go.

Put the roulade on a warmed dish. Stir the cream into the remaining spinach purée and pour around the roulade. Serve immediately.

GARLIC BREAD

SERVES 4-6

INGREDIENTS

1 French loaf

Garlic Butter (page 179), softened

1 tsp mixed fresh herbs,
chopped (optional)

Slice the bread evenly, taking care not to cut right through the bottom of the loaf.

Spread both sides of each slice with the softened Garlic Butter and sprinkle with herbs.

Wrap the loaf in foil and heat through in the oven for about 20 minutes.

BAKED GARLIC CROUTONS

Unlike fried garlic croutons, these can be kept warm in the oven until they are needed. Spread slices of white bread, with the crusts removed, with softened Garlic Butter. Cut into small cubes and arrange, butter side up, on a greased baking tray. Bake at 375°F until crisp and golden.

GARLIC BUNS

Slice the top third off white or whole wheat buns and scoop out most of the crumb. Crumble this and toss it in melted Clarified Garlic Butter with some poppy seeds or mixed herbs. Pile the buttered crumbs into the bun shells, replace the tops and warm through before serving.

GARLIC PULLED BREAD

Use two forks to scoop out the insides of a fresh white loaf in bite-sized pieces, stretching them slightly. Put them on a baking sheet and drizzle with melted Clarified Garlic butter and bake at 375°F until crisped.

POTATO STREAMERS

SERVES 4

INGREDIENTS

2 large potatoes

2 garlic cloves, sliced

¼ cup butter

1 Tbsp Parmesan cheese

salt and freshly ground black pepper

paprika

Preheat the oven to 425°F. Peel the potatoes and cut them into ¾-inch slices. Peel each slice round and round to form a long, thin ribbon.

Soak the ribbons in iced water for at least an hour. Drain them and pat dry with absorbent paper.

Heat the garlic and butter gently in a frying pan until the garlic becomes transparent. Remove the garlic.

Take the pan off the heat, dip each potato streamer into the hot garlic butter, and lay the streamers on a baking pan. When all the streamers have been dipped, sprinkle the Parmesan over them and season with salt, pepper, and a little paprika.

Bake until crisp and well-browned, which should take 7–12 minutes. Serve warm.

COOK'S TIP

Deep fry the dried streamers, drain on paper towels, and sprinkle with garlic salt. Serve immediately.

◀ *Garlic Bread*

GARLIC MILK LOAF

MAKES 1 LARGE LOAF OR 2 SMALL LOAVES

*Add a kick to this traditional country loaf by flavoring it with garlic. Serve warm or toasted,
spread with butter for a delicious snack.*

INGREDIENTS

1 head garlic, about 12 cloves

1¼ cups milk

4½ cups all-purpose flour, warmed

1 tsp salt

2 Tbsp butter, melted

1 Tbsp fresh yeast

½ tsp sugar

1 egg, well beaten

rock salt

a little finely chopped garlic (optional)

Preheat the oven to 450°F. Blanch the separated, unpeeled, garlic cloves in boiling water for 5 minutes.

Drain and peel them, and simmer in the milk for 10–15 minutes, until tender. Then sift the flour with the salt into a large bowl and make a well in the center.

Either sieve or blend the milk and garlic to make a smooth paste, and add the melted butter.

Cream the yeast with the sugar and add to the warm garlic milk with the beaten egg. Pour onto the flour.

Mix the ingredients, thoroughly and knead lightly until smooth. The dough should be soft.

Leave to rise, covered, in a warm place for about 1 hour.

Shape the dough into one large or two small loaves and place on a greased baking sheet. Cut several parallel slashes from end to end of each loaf, and leave to rise for 15 minutes.

Sprinkle each loaf with rock salt and a little chopped garlic, and bake for 20–30 minutes until well browned and hollow-sounding when tapped underneath.

COOK'S TIP

Leave the garlic cloves whole or add ⅓ cup of pine nuts, browned in a little oil, to the dough before leaving it aside to rise.

NEW ORLEANS-STYLE SANDWICH

SERVES 4 ~ 6

Like other Mediterranean-style sandwiches, this is drenched in olive oil with a good whiff of garlic and a few drops of vinegar. Sometimes you can find ready-made olive relish, but making it yourself means you can add as much garlic as you wish, and as much olive oil, too.

INGREDIENTS

5 garlic cloves, chopped

25–35 black olives (such as Kalamata or Italian oil-cured), pitted and sliced

25–35 green pimiento-stuffed olives, sliced

2 roasted, red bell peppers, peeled and cut into strips

3–5 Tbsp chopped fresh parsley

½–¾ cup extra-virgin olive oil or other full-flavored oil

1–2 Tbsp white wine vinegar

several pinches of oregano

1 baguette or other freshly baked, country bread loaf

5–6 oz salami, or more, sliced

5–6 oz mortadella, or more, sliced

5–6 oz prosciutto or Parma ham, or more, sliced

5–6 oz Spanish chorizo sausage, sliced

3 cups thinly sliced, mild cheese (such as Monterey Jack, or fontina)

Combine the garlic with the olives, bell peppers, parsley, olive oil, vinegar, and oregano.

Slice open the bread, and hollow out some of the center of the loaf to make room for the stuffing.

Drizzle the cut sides with some of the oily juices from the olive mixture, then fill the bottom with about ⅔ of the olive salad. Then layer the meats and cheeses, before topping with the rest of the olive mixture. Close up tightly, and chill until ready to eat.

BOCADILLO FROM SANTA GERTRUDIS

SERVES 4

Santa Gertrudis is a little village in the hills of the Mediterranean island of Ibiza.
Try one of these delicious sandwiches for breakfast.

INGREDIENTS

4 large crusty bread rolls, with soft,
tender, slightly sour crumbs

4–8 garlic cloves, cut into halves

extra-virgin olive oil, to drizzle generously

2–3 ripe tomatoes, slightly squished
or thinly sliced

sprinkling of oregano

8–12 slices Parma ham or prosciutto

8–12 slices of manchego or other mild,
white cheese (such as Monterey
Jack or sonoma)

Partially cut, partially break apart the bread rolls lengthwise and lightly toast. Rub the cut garlic on to the toasted cut side of the bread—the coarse edges are slightly sharp and will act as a shredder. If there is any garlic left at the end, just chop and sprinkle it on top.

Drizzle the cut, garlic-rubbed rolls with olive oil, then rub with the tomatoes and sprinkle with oregano. Layer with the ham and cheese, close up, and heat again, preferably in a pan with a heavy weight that will press the bread together as it heats through.

Serve immediately, with a few olives on the side.

Pasta & Grains

PENNE WITH MIXED MUSHROOM SAUCE

SERVES 4

*Sautéed mushrooms and asparagus pieces, simmered in a creamy tomato sauce, then tossed with
quill-shaped penne and fresh basil, make a flavorful, rich Italian pasta.*

INGREDIENTS

1 onion, roughly chopped

4 garlic cloves, roughly chopped

3 Tbsp olive oil or butter, plus a little
extra to finish

12 oz mixed mushrooms, cut into
bite-size pieces

salt and freshly ground black pepper

1 lb fresh tomatoes, finely chopped
(or 1 x 8-oz can chopped tomatoes
including juice)

¼–½ tsp sugar

1½ cups heavy cream

1–2 oz fresh sweet basil, torn

12–16 oz penne

1 bunch thin asparagus, tough ends
broken off, cut into bite-size lengths

4–6 Tbsp shredded Parmesan cheese

In a large frying pan, sauté the onion
and garlic in the olive oil or butter,
until softened. Add the mushrooms
and cook, stirring occasionally to
prevent sticking.

Season with salt and pepper, then
pour in the tomatoes, and add the
sugar. Bring to a boil and cook, stirring,
a few minutes more.

Add the cream and about a third
of the torn basil. Taste, adjust the
seasoning if necessary, and remove the
mixture from the heat.

Cook the pasta in a large pan of
boiling, salted water until half done,
then add the asparagus, and finish
cooking. The pasta should be firm to
the bite and the vegetables just tender.
Drain well.

Toss the hot pasta and asparagus
with the creamy tomato-mushroom
sauce, then toss with the Parmesan
cheese, the remaining basil, and a little
extra olive oil or butter. Serve while
hot on warmed plates.

COOK'S TIP

Make the mushroom mix as interesting
as possible by including pink oyster
mushrooms, chanterelles, shiitakes,
ordinary white mushrooms, porcini,
and trompettes de la mort.

GARLIC DILL PIZZA

SERVES 2 ~ 4

The more garlic you add to this recipe, the more it tastes like garlic bread. Any topping that can be complemented by garlic goes well on this crust. It is great just topped with cheese.

INGREDIENTS

1 package active dry yeast

1 cup warm water

1 tsp dried dill

2 garlic cloves, chopped

2½ cups all-purpose flour, sifted

2 Tbsp olive oil

½ tsp salt

1 cup shredded cheese
(such as Mozzarella or Jack)

In a large bowl, combine the yeast, warm water, dill, garlic, and 1½ cups of the flour. Mix well to blend. Add the oil, salt, and remaining flour and stir until the dough sticks together. Place the dough on a lightly floured surface. Knead the dough for about 5 minutes until it is smooth and elastic. If the dough gets sticky, sprinkle it with a little flour.

Roll the dough into a ball and place it in a lightly oiled bowl. Cover the bowl with a clean towel and set in a warm place to rise for 1 hour until doubled in volume.

When the dough has risen, roll it into a ball to make one 12-inch regular crust pizza or divide it in two balls to make two thin-crust 12-inch pizzas. Allow the dough to rest for 20 minutes.

When ready to bake, place the dough in the center of a lightly oiled pan. Roll outward toward the edges with the palm of your hand until the dough fills the pan evenly. Add the shredded cheese, or topping of your choice and bake in a preheated oven at 450°F for 25–35 minutes.

SPAGHETTI WITH EGGPLANT AND ZUCCHINI

SERVES 4

A very simple recipe becomes something special with the addition of pine nuts and eggplant slices.

INGREDIENTS

olive oil, for frying

⅓ cup pine nuts

1 large eggplant, sliced

1 lb spaghetti

2 large zucchini, sliced

1–2 garlic cloves, crushed

2 Tbsp torn basil leaves and parsley

salt and freshly ground black pepper

freshly shredded Parmesan cheese

Bring a large pan of salted water to a boil. Heat a little oil in a large skillet, add the pine nuts and cook until golden. Remove with a slotted spoon and leave on a plate, then add the eggplant to the skillet with more oil and fry until starting to soften and brown.

Add the pasta to the boiling salted water, return to a boil and simmer until it is still firm to the bite.

Add the zucchini and garlic to the skillet and continue frying for 8–10 minutes until all the vegetables are soft and golden.

Drain the pasta and add it to the skillet with the herbs. Season to taste. Add the pine nuts and toss well. Serve immediately, with shredded Parmesan.

ARTICHOKE WITH MUSHROOM LASAGNE

SERVES 4

Artichockes pair very deliciously with porcini. Both are reminiscent of Mediterranean cuisine, and both are very good when tossed with pasta.

INGREDIENTS

2 artichokes

few drops lemon juice

2–3 oz mixed dried wild mushrooms or 12 oz fresh mushrooms

½ cup hot water, if using dried mushrooms, or stock

1 onion, chopped

4 garlic cloves, roughly chopped

3 Tbsp butter, plus a little extra for buttering the pasta

1 cup light whipping cream

½ cup ricotta cheese or sour cream

salt and freshly ground black pepper

few gratings of nutmeg

8 oz egg lasagne sheets

2 cups shredded cheese (such as Gruyère, Emmentaler, Parmesan, asiago, dried Monteray Jack, or a combination)

Snap the outer leaves from the artichokes by bending them back crisply. When you reach the tender inner leaves, stop, and use a paring knife to trim the base of the artichoke. Slice off the sharp, prickly tops that are left, then cut each artichoke heart into quarters and carefully pare out the thistle-like center.

Blanch the artichoke hearts for about 3 minutes in boiling water to which you have added a squeeze of lemon. Remove, rinse in cold water, and, when cool enough to handle, slice the hearts thickly.

If you are using dried mushrooms, rehydrate them. Remove them from the water, squeeze dry, and cut into bite-size pieces. Reserve the liquid from the mushrooms.

Lightly sauté the onion and garlic in the butter until it is softened, then add the mushrooms and artichoke slices. Raise the heat and sauté, until the vegetables are lightly browned in spots throughout.

Pour in the mushroom liquid or stock, bring to a boil, and then reduce over high heat. Pour in the light whipping cream and cook for a few minutes more.

Lower the heat, stir in the ricotta cheese or sour cream, a few drops of lemon juice, salt and pepper, and nutmeg. Set aside the sauce while you cook the pasta.

Cook the pasta, according to the instructions on the package, until it is just tender. Drain carefully so that you do not break too much of the pasta, then lightly toss with a little butter, and arrange on a platter.

Pour the artichoke and mushroom sauce over, then blanket with the shredded cheese, and toss lightly. Serve immediately.

PASTA WITH TUNA AND TOMATO SAUCE

SERVES 4 ~ 6

The addition of juicy chunks of tuna is characteristic of Italian cooking. Don't worry about using canned tuna as a substitute for fresh, as the canned is actually more authentic, although you could use left-over chunks of broiled tuna in its place.

INGREDIENTS

1 onion, chopped

5 garlic cloves, chopped

6 Tbsp extra-virgin olive oil, or as desired

2½ lb diced tomatoes (or 14-oz can, including the juices)

2 Tbsp tomato paste

salt and freshly ground black pepper

pinch of sugar

pinch of oregano and/or majoram, to taste

6½-oz can tuna, drained

1 lb spaghetti

3 Tbsp capers, preferably salted rather than brined (rinse well if brined)

10–15 black olives, pitted and quartered

3 Tbsp chopped fresh parsley

few Tbsp of toasted bread crumbs (optional)

In a skillet, lightly sauté the onion and garlic in the olive oil until softened, then add the tomatoes and cook over medium heat until the tomatoes are juicy.

Add the tomato paste if needed, then season with salt, pepper, sugar, and oregano or majoram to taste. Add the tuna to the sauce, and heat the mixture through.

Meanwhile, cook the pasta in a saucepan of rapidly boiling, salted water until it is firm to the bite, then drain the pasta.

Pour half the sauce into the pasta, and toss together with the capers and olives, then toss again with the rest of the sauce.

Sprinkle with the parsley and the bread crumbs (if using), and serve this dish immediately.

CHICKEN AND EGGPLANT RISOTTO

SERVES 4

A good risotto should be moist, and the rice should still have a little bite in the middle.
Serve the eggplant as a sauce on top of the risotto—it works very well indeed.

INGREDIENTS

1 large eggplant

1 Tbsp lemon juice

good pinch of saffron strands

5 cups well-flavored chicken broth

3 Tbsp olive oil

1 large onion, finely chopped

2–3 celery sticks, finely sliced

2 chicken breast fillets, finely diced

2 garlic cloves, finely sliced

1½ cups arborio rice

2 Tbsp fresh flat-leaf parsley

salt and freshly ground black pepper

1 Tbsp fresh tomato paste or
ketchup, optional

⅔ cup dry white wine

2–3 tomatoes, skinned, seeded,
and chopped

Cook the eggplant over a barbecue, under a moderate broiler, or in a hot oven until the skin is wrinkled and blistered and the flesh is tender. Turn once or twice during cooking. Cover with a damp cloth and leave for about 10 minutes to cool slightly, then peel off the skin. Plunge the flesh into a bowl of water with a tablespoon of lemon juice, to prevent discoloration, and leave until required.

Soak the pinch of saffron strands in the hot broth.

Heat the olive oil in a large skillet over a moderate heat, add the onion and celery, and cook until soft but not browned, then add the chicken. Cook over a slightly higher heat until the chicken is white all over, then add the garlic and the rice, tossing them in the skillet juices.

Add about one-third of the broth to the skillet, then bring to a boil, and simmer, stirring frequently, until all the broth has been absorbed. Add half the remaining broth and repeat the simmering process.

Drain the eggplant and squeeze with your hands, extracting as much liquid as possible, then chop the flesh roughly and blend it with the parsley and seasoning to a smooth paste. Add 1 tablespoon of tomato paste or ketchup for color.

Stir the wine into the risotto, then add the remaining broth and continue cooking until it has a creamy consistency. Add the chopped tomatoes just before the risotto is ready, and season to taste with salt and black pepper.

CHICKEN AND OLIVE RISOTTO

SERVES 4

Full of chicken, tomatoes, and olives, this rice dish is a classic
of the Sicilian table.

INGREDIENTS

½ onion, chopped

4 garlic cloves, chopped

3 Tbsp extra-virgin olive oil

2 cups arborio rice

12–14 oz diced tomatoes, fresh or
canned, with their juices

½ cup dry white wine

1¾ pints chicken broth, or as needed

25 green olives, pimiento-stuffed, or about
15 black and 15 green olives, stoned and
cut into halves

1 chicken breast, poached, and cut into
shreds or small pieces

several pinches of mixed Italian herbs, or

a combination of rosemary,
thyme, and sage

freshly ground black pepper

3–4 oz Romano or other sharp cheese,
shredded coarsely

1–2 Tbsp chopped fresh parsley

In a large frying pan, lightly sauté the onion and garlic in the olive oil until softened.

Stir in the rice and cook for a few minutes until lightly golden, then add the tomatoes and cook for a few more minutes.

Pour in the wine, and stir until the rice has absorbed the wine. Begin to add the broth, a few half-cups at a time, letting the rice absorb the liquid while you stir, and increasing the amounts while the rice cooks so that the liquid is absorbed more quickly.

When the rice is firm to the bite, stir in the olives, chicken, herbs, pepper (the olives and the Romano are both salty, so you probably won't need salt), cheese, and parsley. Serve immediately.

PASTA WITH RAW TOMATO SAUCE

SERVES 4

This recipe is a classic Neapolitan combination of hot pasta with raw tomatoes, rich with olive oil,
basil, garlic, and a crumbling of goat's cheese for fresh piquancy.

INGREDIENTS

10 very ripe, juicy tomatoes, diced

salt

few drops of balsamic vinegar

3 garlic cloves, chopped

4–6 Tbsp extra-virgin olive oil

several handfuls of fresh basil,
torn coarsely

few pinches of hot-pepper flakes

12 oz pasta of choice

1 cup goat's cheese, crumbled

In a large bowl, combine the tomatoes with several pinches of salt, the balsamic vinegar, the garlic, most of the olive oil (except for 1 tablespoon for tossing the cooked pasta), and the basil (plus the chile flakes, if using). Leave in the refrigerator for several hours or at least for 30 minutes.

When ready to serve, cook the pasta until it is firm to the bite, then drain and toss with the goat's cheese and remaining olive oil. Add to the sauce, and serve immediately.

SPAGHETTI WITH TOMATO AND CLAM SAUCE

SERVES 4

Tiny clams are tossed on a sea of tomato-based spaghetti sauce, with a dusting of fine, green parsley, and the heady scent of garlic. Be careful not to swallow the shells; larger clams are more convenient. If clams are not available, use mussels.

INGREDIENTS

2¼ lb fresh clams in their shells, or mussels (removed from shells)

8 garlic cloves, chopped

½ cup strong-flavored, extra-virgin olive oil

several pinches of hot, red-pepper flakes, or ½–1 dried, red chile, crushed

½ cup dry white wine

1 cup puréed tomatoes

1 Tbsp tomato paste

sea salt to taste

pinch of sugar

several large pinches of dried oregano, crumbled

1 lb spaghetti

2–3 Tbsp chopped fresh parsley

Cover the clams or mussels with cold, salted water, and leave for 30–60 minutes to clean. Remove from the water and drain.

Sauté the clams or mussels with half the garlic in the olive oil for about 5 minutes, then add the hot pepper flakes and wine. Cook over a high heat until the sauce begins to evaporate.

Add the puréed tomatoes, tomato paste, the remaining garlic, salt, sugar (to taste), and oregano. Cover and cook over medium heat for about 10 minutes or until the clams have all popped open.

Cook the spaghetti until it is firm to the bite, then drain and toss with a few tablespoons of the sauce. Pour it on to a large platter or into bowls, and top with the remaining sauce and clams. Sprinkle with parsley and serve.

RAVIOLI

SERVES 4

As the amount of filling you put into each ravioli and the size you cut them out
can vary so much, the amounts given per ½ quantity of the Garlic Pasta
recipe (see page 80) are only a guide.

INGREDIENTS

8 oz spinach purée

2 garlic cloves, minced

¾ cup cream cheese or
low-fat soft cheese

2 Tbsp Parmesan cheese

I small egg, well beaten

salt and freshly ground black pepper

½ quantity of Garlic Pasta dough

Combine the spinach purée, garlic, cheese, and beaten egg. Season with salt and pepper to taste and leave on one side.

On a floured surface, roll and stretch the pasta dough repeatedly until it is as thin as possible. Leave for 15 minutes to firm up a little.

Brush half of the dough sheet with water and put teaspoonfuls of the filling on the wetted half, spacing it 1–1½ inches apart.

Fold over the other half of the dough and press down firmly round each little mound of filling.

Cut between the ravioli shapes with a sharp knife or pastry wheel to make squares of pasta with a mound of filling in each.

Boil the ravioli in lots of salted water for 5–7 minutes or until the pasta is just cooked and the filling heated through.

Drain and toss with a little butter and serve immediately, with extra butter and Parmesan cheese, and perhaps a little cream.

MUSHROOM-RICOTTA AND SAUSAGE CANNELLONI

SERVES 4

Diced, sautéed mushrooms added to ricotta cheese make delicious cannelloni. If dried porcini are not available, use ordinary common cultivated mushrooms, 8–10 ounces, diced and sautéed, instead.

INGREDIENTS

3½ oz dried mushrooms (such as porcini)

1 cup water

2 plump Italian sausages, roughly chopped

5–10 fresh common cultivated mushrooms, diced

5 garlic cloves, chopped

1½ cups of ricotta cheese

6 Tbsp freshly shredded Parmesan cheese

1 egg, lightly beaten

salt and freshly ground black pepper

several pinches of thyme and/or rosemary, as desired

8 egg-roll wrappers or fresh pasta

2 lb fresh ripe tomatoes, diced (or 1 x 21-oz can chopped tomatoes with their juice)

6 oz Mozzarella cheese, shredded

several handfuls fresh basil leaves, roughly torn

Place the dried mushrooms and the water in a saucepan and bring to a boil. Reduce the heat and simmer for about 5 minutes, then cover, and leave to plump up. When softened, remove the mushrooms from the pan and squeeze, saving the liquid. Roughly chop the mushrooms and strain the mushroom liquid.

Meanwhile, cook the sausages with the fresh mushrooms until lightly browned in spots. Remove from the heat and mix with the garlic, rehydrated mushrooms, ricotta cheese, half the shredded Parmesan cheese, the egg, salt and pepper, and the thyme and/or rosemary.

Preheat the oven to 375°F. Place several tablespoons of the mixture onto one edge of each pasta square, then roll each into a cylinder. Layer the cannelloni in the bottom of a 9 x 12-inch baking dish.

Pour the diced tomatoes over the top, along with the mushroom liquid, then sprinkle with the Mozzarella and remaining Parmesan cheese.

Bake in the oven for 35–40 minutes, until the pasta is cooked, the liquid has been absorbed, and the cheese has melted. Leave to stand a few moments, then serve, with the torn basil leaves scattered over.

GRATIN OF MACARONI WITH
WILD MUSHROOMS AND PEAS

SERVES 4

Mushrooms and pasta are natural partners and make wonderful gratins. Add any sort of bright vegetable
for variety and interest. Artichokes or asparagus can be used instead of the peas.

INGREDIENTS

2 oz small elbow macaroni

8 oz baby peas, fresh or frozen

salt

8–12 oz mixed fresh wild mushrooms, or
a mixture of ordinary white mushrooms
and rehydrated dried mushrooms, diced

3 shallots, chopped

3 garlic cloves, chopped

3 Tbsp butter

3 Tbsp snipped fresh chives

freshly ground black pepper

3–4 Tbsp heavy cream

4–6 Tbsp each shredded fontina
(or Gruyère, asiago, mild white Cheddar,
or Monterey Jack) and Parmesan cheese

Preheat the oven to 375°F. Cook the pasta in rapidly boiling salted water until it is about half tender, then remove from the heat, and drain. Toss with the peas. The pasta should not be cooked so that it becomes soft, and the peas should be still bright green and perhaps a little crunchy.

In a large skillet, sauté the mushrooms, shallots, and garlic in the butter until the mushrooms are lightly browned. Remove the pan from the heat, and add the chives. Toss the vegetables with the pasta and peas. Season to taste.

Layer half the pasta mixture in the base of a gratin or casserole dish, then drizzle with half the cream and half the cheese. Top with the remaining cheese, pouring the other half of the cream over the top.

Bake in the oven for 20 minutes, or until the pasta is heated through and the cheese has melted. If the pasta seems dry, add a little more cream. Serve immediately.

GARLIC PASTA

SERVES 6

Keep this dish simple or use the dough to make ravioli (see page 77).

INGREDIENTS

4½ cups all-purpose flour

2 eggs

1 Tbsp olive oil

juice of 2–3 garlic cloves

2 Tbsp well-drained spinach purée or
1 Tbsp tomato paste

1 tsp salt

tepid water to mix

4 Tbsp butter

Parmesan cheese

Mix together the flour, eggs, oil, garlic juice, spinach or tomato paste, salt, and add enough tepid water to make a stiff dough.

Knead on a well-floured surface for at least 10 minutes or until it is elastic.

Divide the dough in half. Roll and stretch each piece repeatedly until it is as thin as possible. Leave for 15 minutes to firm up a little.

Sprinkle each dough sheet with a little flour, roll up loosely, and slice into ribbons ¼–½ inch wide with a sharp knife.

Boil in plenty of salted water for 3–6 minutes until just done, then drain, and serve immediately with butter and Parmesan cheese, or whatever sauce you fancy.

NEAPOLITAN PIZZA

SERVES 4

Garlic and anchovies combine to create a genuine south Italian flavor.

INGREDIENTS

2¼ cups all-purpose flour, sifted

1 Tbsp fresh yeast

½ tsp sugar

tepid water to mix

½ tsp salt

2¼ cups/1½ lb ripe tomatoes, skinned, seeded, and coarsely chopped

freshly ground black pepper

2 tsp finely chopped fresh basil

2–3 garlic cloves, finely chopped

12 anchovy fillets

6 oz Mozzarella cheese, thinly sliced

1½ Tbsp olive oil

Preheat the oven to 450°F. Put the sifted flour into a large bowl and make a well in the middle.

Mix the fresh yeast, sugar and 2 tablespoons of the tepid water in a cup and pour into the flour.

Add the salt and mix well, adding tepid water to make a stiff dough.

Knead on a well-floured board until light and elastic. Cover with a clean towel and leave in a warm place for 2–2½ hours until the dough has doubled in size.

Roll the dough into a circle ¼ inch thick, and put it onto a large, well-oiled baking sheet. Leave for 10 minutes.

Top with the tomatoes, plenty of pepper, garlic, and basil followed by the anchovies and sliced Mozzarella cheese. Finally, sprinkle olive oil over the top of the pizza.

Bake for 25–35 minutes in the oven, until the dough is cooked and the cheese bubbles.

MASSAIA MIA

SERVES 2 ~ 3

INGREDIENTS

4 oz prosciutto or cooked ham, diced

1 small garlic clove, crushed

2 Tbsp butter

8 oz fresh pink or green tagliatelle

3 Tbsp green peas, cooked

3 Tbsp light or cereal cream

salt and freshly ground black pepper

2 Tbsp Parmesan cheese, to serve

1 Tbsp chopped parsley, to serve

In a skillet, gently heat the diced prosciutto or ham and garlic in the butter. Add the tagliatelle to boiling salted water and cook for 3–5 minutes or until just tender.

Drain the pasta and add the prosciutto or ham, garlic butter, peas, and cream, and season with salt and pepper to taste.

Just before serving, sprinkle with Parmesan and parsley.

COOK'S TIP

Heat the garlic in the butter and stir into the hot, drained pasta, together with 4 oz of diced smoked salmon.

RED BEANS AND RICE WITH TASSO AND ANDOUILLE

SERVES 6 ~ 8

The use of two highly spiced meats means this is a very spicy dish. You can use ham hocks instead of the Tasso, but increase the amount of cayenne and black pepper, or the end result will be very mild. The addition of vegetables at the end adds crunch.

INGREDIENTS

2 cups dried kidney beans, picked over

2–4 Tbsp vegetable oil

2 large chopped onions

1½ cups chopped celery

1½ cups chopped green bell pepper

2 garlic cloves, chopped

8 oz Tasso, cubed

8 oz Andouille sausage, sliced

2 bay leaves

2 tsp salt

2 tsp ground cumin

1 tsp dry mustard

1 Tbsp fresh oregano, chopped

¼ tsp freshly ground black pepper

¼ tsp cayenne

1 cup chopped green onion

½ cup chopped celery

½ cup chopped green bell pepper

¼ cup chopped fresh parsley

5–6 cups cooked rice, to serve

In 5 quarts water, soak the beans for at least 4 hours or overnight. Drain, rinse, and return to the large pot with 6 cups water. Bring to a boil, then reduce the heat and simmer, skimming the foam, while you prepare the vegetables.

Meanwhile, heat the oil in a skillet and sauté the onion, 1½ cups celery, 1½ cups green bell pepper and the garlic until wilted. Unless you use a very large skillet, it is easier to sauté the vegetables in two batches. Add the vegetables to the beans, along with the Tasso, sausage, herbs, and seasoning and continue simmering, stirring occasionally, for 1–1½ hours or until tender. Add extra water if necessary. Taste and adjust seasoning.

Just before serving, stir in the remaining green onions, celery, green bell pepper, and parsley and mix well. Serve over rice.

MUSHROOMS AND BARLEY WITH NEW ORLEANS SPICES

SERVES 4

This Cajun-style treatment for mushrooms and barley is very comforting and tasty. Serve as a side dish for barbecued meat or fish or as a vegetarian main course.

INGREDIENTS

8 oz barley

3¾ cups stock

2 oz dried mushrooms, any kind, broken into small pieces

2 Tbsp olive oil

I onion, chopped

5 garlic cloves, chopped

½ each green and red bell peppers, chopped

2 fresh ripe tomatoes, chopped

I small, hot dried red chile, or to taste, crumbled into flakes

½ tsp each ground cumin, thyme, and paprika

salt and freshly ground black pepper

Place the barley in a saucepan with the stock. Bring to a boil, then reduce the heat, and simmer for about 40 minutes or until tender. If the barley gets too dry, add more liquid. If it is too soupy, add more barley early on, or cook the mixture over a higher heat for longer, letting the liquid evaporate.

During the last 20 minutes of cooking, add the dried mushrooms.

Heat the olive oil in a skillet and lightly sauté the onion until softened, then stir in the garlic, and green and red bell peppers, and cook for about 5 minutes or until softened. Add the tomatoes, red chile, cumin, thyme, and paprika, and cook over high heat until the tomatoes become thick and mushy.

Toss the onion mixture with the barley, season and serve.

FISH &
SEAFOOD

TUNA AND EGGPLANT KABOBS

SERVES 4

These are perfect kabobs for the garden or beach barbecue or to broil indoors

when the season changes.

INGREDIENTS

1 lb fresh tuna steaks, about 1 inch thick,
cut into 1-inch cubes

1 long, thin, Japanese-style eggplant

MARINADE

grated zest and juice of 1 lime

4 Tbsp olive oil

1 garlic clove, minced

2 Tbsp chopped fresh oregano and parsley

salt and freshly ground black pepper

Place the tuna in a glass bowl, then add all the marinade ingredients. Stir well and leave for at least 1 hour, stirring once or twice.

Half cook the eggplant on the barbecue or under the broiler, until the skin is just starting to wrinkle. Cut into ½-inch thick slices. Thread the tuna and eggplant onto skewers, then brush with the remaining marinade.

Cook over a moderate heat for 5–6 minutes on each side, either on the barbecue or under a broiler, basting with any remaining marinade. Serve with a rice salad.

SMOKED HADDOCK LASAGNE

SERVES 6 ~ 8

An interesting alternative to vegetarian or meat lasagne, the strong flavor of smoked
haddock perfectly complements this traditional Italian dish.

INGREDIENTS

12 garlic cloves, unpeeled

1½ lb smoked haddock fillets

1¼ cups milk

pinch of saffron threads (optional)

½ bay leaf

1 medium onion, thinly sliced

4 Tbsp butter

4 Tbsp all-purpose flour

1 Tbsp Parmesan cheese

3 hard-cooked eggs

salt and freshly ground black pepper

12 oz dry green lasagne

a little oil

1¼ cups/12 oz ripe tomatoes, skinned
and thinly sliced

1 tsp chopped fresh basil

1½ cups Mozzarella cheese, thinly sliced

Preheat the oven to 425°F. Plunge the unpeeled garlic cloves into boiling water and simmer for 20–25 minutes, until soft. Drain, peel, and mash.

Poach the fish in the milk with the saffron (if used) and the bay leaf for about 10 minutes or until the flesh is firm and flakes easily.

Lift the fish carefully out of the milk, skin if necessary, and break into bite-sized pieces with a fork.

Sweat the onion in the butter until transparent, taking care not to let it brown. Stir in the flour and cook for several minutes more. Discard the bay leaf and any bits of fish skin, add the milk a little at a time and let the sauce simmer for 5 minutes.

Remove from the heat and stir in the Parmesan cheese, mashed garlic, fish pieces, and the hard-cooked eggs cut into eighths. Season well with salt and pepper and leave, covered, in a cool place until needed.

Boil the lasagne in batches in lots of salted water with a little oil to stop the sheets from sticking together. They should take 10–20 minutes to cook until they are firm to the bite.

Lift each piece of cooked pasta out and run under cold water and lay on a damp dish cloth.

When all the pieces of lasagne are cooked, use some of them to line the bottom and sides of a well-greased

small, deep roasting pan or large pie plate, and spread over them half the fish mixture.

Top with half of the tomatoes, sprinkled with half the basil. Add another layer of pasta, fish, tomatoes, and basil, finishing with a layer of pasta on the top.

Spread the sliced Mozzarella over the top and bake for approximately 30 minutes until the top is crisped and well browned.

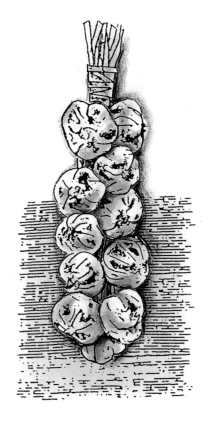

EGGPLANT AND COD BAKE

SERVES 4

A simple bake with the flavors of the Mediterranean. Serve this with a crisp green salad and crusty French bread to mop up the juices.

INGREDIENTS

butter for greasing

2–3 Tbsp olive oil

I eggplant, sliced

I large onion, finely sliced

I garlic clove, crushed

2 Tbsp capers

⅓ cup black olives, pitted

2 cups chopped canned tomatoes

I Tbsp chopped mixed fresh herbs,
such as parsley, oregano, marjoram

salt and freshly ground black pepper

I½ lb cod fillet, skinned

Preheat the oven to 400°F. Butter an 8-inch ovenproof serving dish. Heat 2–3 tablespoons of oil in a large skillet and fry the eggplant slices gently until tender but not brown. Drain on absorbent paper towels. Add a little more oil if necessary, then add the onion and cook until softened and just starting to brown. Stir in the garlic, capers, and olives, then add the tomatoes and herbs, and season to taste. Simmer the sauce for 5 minutes, until it is slightly thickened and the onions are cooked.

Pour the tomato sauce into the prepared dish. Divide the cod into 4 portions and add to the sauce. Cover the fish with the fried eggplant slices and dot with butter. Place the dish on a baking sheet if it seems very full and likely to bubble over, then bake in the hot oven for 20 minutes, until the eggplant slices are browned. Serve immediately.

QUENELLES WITH PINK FENNEL SAUCE

SERVES 4 ~ 6

This may be fiddly to prepare but the result is certainly worth the effort.

INGREDIENTS

1½ lb white fish fillets

2 garlic cloves, finely crushed

1¼ cups water

½ tsp salt

½ cup butter

1 cup all-purpose flour, sifted

2 eggs and 2 egg whites

2 Tbsp chilled light or cereal cream

salt and freshly ground black pepper

fish stock or water

8-oz head fennel

1 Tbsp finely chopped onion

2 Tbsp white wine

¾ cup/8 oz tomatoes, skinned, seeded, and chopped

½ tsp sugar

12 oz green tagliatelle or fettucine

1½ tsp fennel seeds

Blend the fish to a smooth purée with the garlic and refrigerate. Bring the water, salt, and half the butter to a boil. When the butter has melted, remove from the heat and tip in the sifted flour.

Beat over a moderate heat until the mixture leaves the sides of the pan and forms a mass.

Remove from the heat and beat in the eggs and the extra whites, one at a time. Turn into a large mixing bowl and add the raw fish and garlic purée. Beat in the cream, and season with salt and pepper to taste.

Form into 16 quenelles using two wetted serving spoons. Fill one spoon with the mixture and use the other to round the top.

Poach the quenelles as soon as they are all shaped, in a deep frying pan of barely simmering fish stock or water for 15–20 minutes. Lift them out, cover with a piece of greased foil, and keep warm.

To make the sauce, chop the fennel finely, and sweat it with the onion, wine, and half the remaining butter until tender.

Mix in the chopped tomatoes and sugar, and blend to a smooth purée.

Season with salt and pepper to taste and keep warm.

Cook the pasta in lightly salted boiling water until it still has bite, drain, toss in the remaining butter and the fennel seeds, and put in a heated serving dish.

Arrange the warm quenelles on the pasta, pour over the sauce, and serve.

COOK'S TIP

The quenelle mixture can also be served as individual fish mousses. Pack into well-buttered individual soufflé dishes or ramekins, set them in a roasting pan, half-full of boiling water, and bake at 350°F until the mousses have risen and drawn away from the sides of their dishes.

STUFFED MUSSELS

SERVES 4

The best mussels for stuffing are the large, green-lipped variety.

INGREDIENTS

20 large green-lipped mussels,
on the half shell

4 Tbsp olive oil

1 large onion, finely chopped

1 red chile, deseeded and very
finely chopped

1 small eggplant, very finely chopped

2 garlic cloves, crushed

salt and freshly ground black pepper

¾ cup fresh whole wheat bread crumbs

flat-leaf parsley sprigs, to garnish

Preheat the oven to 425°F. Loosen the mussels on the half shells and arrange them on a cookie sheet.

Heat the oil in a large skillet. Add the onion and chile and cook until starting to soften, then add the eggplant and garlic. Continue cooking for 5–6 minutes, until all the vegetables are soft and lightly browned. Season well, then add the bread crumbs and mix thoroughly.

Pile a teaspoonful of filling into each shell over the mussel, then bake for 12–15 minutes, until piping hot. Serve immediately, garnished with sprigs of flat-leaf parsley.

TANDOORI SOLE

SERVES 4

You can use any firm white fish for this dish.

INGREDIENTS

2 tsp cumin

½ tsp turmeric

½ tsp cloves

½ tsp cardamom seeds

½ tsp chile powder

½ tsp freshly ground black pepper

½ tsp yellow mustard seeds

1 medium onion, chopped

2 garlic cloves, finely chopped

1 cup natural unsweetened yogurt

6 fillets of sole, skinned

Preheat the oven to 350°F. Grind the spices together and blend them with the onion and garlic. Mix the spice mixture into the yogurt.

Place the fish in a shallow dish and pour over the spice and yogurt mixture. Leave to marinate for about 6 hours.

Remove the fish from the marinade, wrap it in kitchen foil and bake for 30 minutes.

COOK'S TIP

This recipe can be used for chicken. Double the amount of yogurt, leave to marinate for 12 hours, and cook for 1 hour.

STEAMED LANGOUSTINES

SERVES 4

Cooked over open coals or steamed gently, langoustines are luscious when served with nothing more than garlic, lemon juice, and lots of olive oil.

INGREDIENTS

1½ lb fresh langoustine or jumbo shrimp in their shells

½ cup extra-virgin olive oil

juice of 2 lemons

salt to taste

1 garlic clove, minced

1 bunch flat-leaf parsley, chopped

Place the langoustines or shrimp in a steamer, and cook them until they have turned red, which will take about 10 minutes for langoustine, 5 minutes for shrimp.

Whisk together the olive oil and lemon juice, then whisk in the salt, garlic, and chopped parsley.

Serve the sauce on the side, or a little spooned over the warm seafood, and the rest in a bowl on the side for dipping. Serve immediately, along with a bowl for the discarded shells.

LIME-MARINATED SWORDFISH WITH EGGPLANT RIBBONS

SERVES 4

Swordfish readily absorbs the flavors of marinades. Use lime for a really fresh tang.
Ribbons of fried eggplant provide a striking contrast to the fish.

INGREDIENTS

4 swordfish steaks, about ½ inch
thick and each weighing about 5 oz

3 Tbsp olive oil

I small long eggplant, halved and sliced
into fine ribbons

MARINADE

grated zest and juice of 2 limes

3 Tbsp fruity olive oil

3 scallions, finely chopped

salt and freshly ground black pepper

I garlic clove, minced

I Tbsp fresh parsley, chopped

Mix all the ingredients for the marinade in a shallow dish, then add the swordfish. Leave to marinate for 1 to 4 hours, turning the steaks in the mixture once or twice.

Heat the oil in a large skillet. Drain the swordfish, reserving the marinade, then fry it quickly in the hot oil, allowing 2 to 3 minutes on each side. Remove the fish from the skillet and keep it warm.

Add the marinade to the skillet and heat it gently, then add the eggplant ribbons and cook quickly until they are soft and beginning to brown. Arrange the ribbons on the swordfish steaks before serving, spooning any remaining juices over the fish.

RED MULLET WITH GARLIC

SERVES 6

Tiny red mullet are best used this recipe, but if they are not available,
use a large one and cut it up at the table.

INGREDIENTS

6 Tbsp very finely chopped freshly parsley

6 garlic cloves, minced

salt and freshly ground black pepper

6 small red mullet, cleaned

flour for coating

olive oil for shallow frying

chopped fresh parsley, to garnish

lemon wedges, to serve

In a bowl, combine the parsley with the garlic, and season with salt and freshly ground black pepper.

Place about 1 teaspoon of the garlic mixture into the cavity of each fish and rub any remaining mixture evenly over the skins. Coat the entire surface of the fish lightly and evenly with flour.

Heat the oil in a deep skillet and cook the fish, no more than 2 at a time, for 5–7 minutes, or until crisp on the outside and cooked through. Using a slotted spoon, transfer the fish to a dish lined with absorbent paper towels to drain. Sprinkle with parsley and serve with lemon wedges.

SHRIMP BAKE

SERVES 6 ~ 8

This dish is far better without the addition of extra salt during cooking, as this tends to toughen
the delicate texture of the shrimp. If you find that the salt from the feta cheese is not sufficient
for your taste, then only add more at the table.

INGREDIENTS

3 Tbsp olive oil

2 large onions, grated

2 garlic cloves, minced

3 Tbsp chopped fresh parsley

1 Tbsp chopped fresh dill

pinch of dry mustard

pinch of sugar

15-oz can chopped tomatoes

1 Tbsp tomato paste

1 lb fresh shrimp, shelled and deveined

8 oz feta cheese, crumbled

chopped fresh dill, to garnish

Preheat the oven to 425°F. Heat the olive oil in a large saucepan and sauté the onions for about 5 minutes, or until softened and beginning to brown. Add the garlic, chopped fresh herbs, dry mustard, sugar, chopped tomatoes, and tomato paste to the saucepan.

Simmer the mixture, uncovered, for about 30 minutes, or until the sauce has reduced and thickened slightly.

Add the shrimp to the sauce in the saucepan and stir. Continue to cook for a further 3–5 minutes, or until all the shrimp have turned pink and are cooked through.

Pour the mixture into an ovenproof serving dish and scatter over the crumbled feta cheese. Bake for 5–10 minutes, or until the cheese has melted. Serve immediately, sprinkled with chopped fresh dill.

HONEY GARLIC SHRIMP

SERVES 4

INGREDIENTS

1½ lb large, raw shrimp

3 garlic cloves, minced

juice of 2 lemons

2 tsp sugar

1 Tbsp soy sauce

2 Tbsp olive oil

freshly ground black pepper

1 cup all-purpose flour

2 pinches salt

1 egg

⅔ cup milk and water, mixed

2 Tbsp honey

1-inch root ginger, minced

2 tsp cornstarch

1 Tbsp sesame seeds

Peel the shrimp and cut deeply along the back of each with a sharp knife, removing the main vein. Place them in a shallow dish.

Combine the crushed garlic, lemon juice, sugar, soy sauce, half the oil, and a good shake of black pepper. Pour the mixture over the shrimp and leave to marinate in the refrigerator or in a cool place for 2–4 hours.

Make the batter by sifting together the flour and salt. Add the egg, the remaining oil, and finally the milk and water mixture, a little at a time, until the batter will coat the back of a spoon. Store in the refrigerator.

Drain the shrimp and reserve the marinade. Dip each shrimp in the batter and deep fry for 1½ minutes in very hot fat until crisp and golden.

Drain the shrimp on absorbent kitchen towels and keep warm in a serving dish.

Heat the remaining marinade with the honey, minced ginger, and cornstarch. Stir constantly until the sauce thickens. Allow to simmer, still stirring, for several minutes.

Pour the sauce over the shrimp and turn them gently in it until well coated. Sprinkle with the sesame seeds and serve immediately.

GARLIC GRAVAD LAX

SERVES 6 ~ 8

This cut salmon is ideal for a buffet lunch or dinner as it can be prepared in advance and makes an attractive addition to the table.

INGREDIENTS

2 lb middle-cut salmon

4 garlic cloves, minced

⅓ cup salt

⅓ cup sugar

handful of fresh dill, chopped

Split the salmon into two halves, remove the bone, but leave the skin on.

Mix together all the remaining ingredients in a large bowl.

Place one half of the salmon, skin side down, on a large, flat serving dish and cover with half the mixture. Put the other half of the salmon over it

and top with the remaining mixture.

Weight down the salmon with a plate and leave in a cool place or refrigerator for at least 24 hours. Scrape off the mixture and serve the salmon cut into thin slices.

Serve with a sour cream, mustard, and horseradish dressing with a little fresh dill added.

MIDDLE EASTERN-STYLE BROILED SWORDFISH

SERVES 4

Eaten throughout the Mediterranean, swordfish is usually marinated with bay leaves, lemon, and lots of olive oil, then skewered and cooked over a wood fire.

INGREDIENTS

2½ lb swordfish

1 onion, minced

8 garlic cloves, chopped

juice of 2 lemons

½ cup extra-virgin olive oil

several bay leaves

salt and freshly ground black pepper

TAHINI SAUCE

¾ cup sesame paste (tahini)

2 garlic cloves, chopped

few dashes of hot-pepper sauce

few pinches of cumin

salt and pepper

juice of 1 lemon

2 Tbsp extra-virgin olive oil

½ cup water, or enough to make the consistency of a smooth, thick sauce

few sprigs fresh oregano

lemon wedges, to garnish

In a large bowl, combine the fish, onion, garlic, lemon juice, olive oil, bay leaves, salt, and pepper. Marinate for at least 1 hour, preferably overnight, in the refrigerator.

Cut the fish into cubes and skewer it with the bay leaves on either soaked bamboo (30 minutes in cold water) or on metal skewers, alternating the fish cubes with the bay leaves. Though you don't eat the bay leaves, they perfume the fish delightfully.

Cook the fish over a medium-low charcoal fire for about 8 minutes, turning once or twice to cook evenly.

Meanwhile, make the sauce. Mix the tahini with the garlic, hot-pepper sauce, cumin, salt, pepper, lemon juice, and olive oil, then slowly stir in the water until it has the desired consistency. Taste for seasoning.

Serve the broiled fish kabobs with fresh oregano, accompanied by lemon wedges and the tahini sauce to the side of the skewers.

STIR-FRIED SEAFOOD WITH MINT, GARLIC, AND CHILES

SERVES 4

Although it takes some time to prepare the ingredients, it only takes a few minutes
to cook this dish, so don't be put off by the list and enjoy!

INGREDIENTS

4 oz fish fillets

6 mussels

I small uncooked crab, cleaned and chopped

4 oz squid pieces

4 oz uncooked shrimp

4 oz scallops

2 garlic cloves, chopped

2 large fresh chile peppers, chopped

I Tbsp chopped cilantro roots

I Tbsp vegetable oil

2 Tbsp oyster sauce

2 Tbsp Nuoc Mam sauce, or light soy sauce and I tsp anchovy sauce, mixed well

I sweet bell pepper, cut in strips

I onion, thinly sliced

2 shallots, thinly sliced

4 Tbsp chopped fresh mint

Wash and prepare the seafood. Cut the fish fillets into bite-sized pieces. Scrub the mussels and remove the beards. Take the limbs off the crab and crack the shell with a hammer so the meat is easy to remove at the table. Remove the outer shell, clean out the crab body, and break into bite-size pieces. Set aside.

Put the garlic, chiles, and cilantro root in a blender and make a coarse paste. Put to one side.

Heat the oil and fry the garlic, chile, and cilantro over medium heat. Add the seafood and stir-fry gently so the fish fillet does not break up. Add the oyster sauce and Nuoc Mam sauce. Taste, cover, and simmer the mixture for a few minutes.

Remove the lid and add the sweet bell pepper, onion, shallots, and mint, and stir-fry gently (the fish fillets are now even more delicate) for a couple of minutes, then remove the fish mixture from the heat.

Arrange on a large, shallow serving dish and garnish with mint or whatever herbs you happen to have around. Serve with a large bowl of steaming rice.

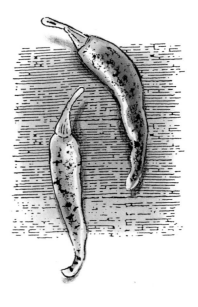

MOROCCAN WHOLE FISH
BAKED WITH CUMIN

SERVES 4

The spicy mixture of cumin, cilantro, and garlic, all bound up in olive oil, makes a delicious flavoring for fish. It is used here on a whole fish for roasting, but you could also use it on pieces of fish wrapped in baking parchment, then roasted in their own steam and juices, or as a paste for portions of fish to be steamed.

INGREDIENTS

1 whole fish, such as a striped bass or snapper, about 3–3½ lb, cleaned but with head and tail left on

1 Tbsp coarse salt

1 lemon, cut into halves (one for juice, and one to cut in wedges for a garnish)

½ cup extra-virgin olive oil

3 Tbsp ground cumin

2 Tbsp paprika

¼ cup chopped fresh cilantro

5 garlic cloves, chopped

freshly ground black pepper

Preheat the oven to 400°F. Wash the fish, then cut slashes on its outside skin. Rub half the salt and lemon juice into the cuts and inside the fish. Leave to sit for 15–25 minutes. Rinse with cold water, and dry with a paper towel.

Combine the olive oil, cumin, paprika, cilantro, garlic, pepper, and remaining salt, and mix into a paste. Rub the paste over the skin of the fish, inside and out, also inside the slashes.

Place the fish on a baking sheet and roast for 30–40 minutes, or until the fish is done; its flesh will feel firm but not hard. Take care not to overcook.

Serve hot, accompanied by wedges of lemon, and a cruet of olive oil if desired, for drizzling.

SALT COD FRITTERS WITH GARLIC

SERVES 6 ~ 8

Salt cod is generally available from delicatessens. Remember to start this recipe a day in advance because the salt cod needs soaking for 24 hours.

INGREDIENTS

1½ lb salt cod, soaked in cold water for 24 hours, with frequent changes of water

¾ cup all-purpose flour

salt and freshly ground black pepper

1 Tbsp olive oil

⅔ cup warm water

1 egg white

olive oil for deep frying

lemon wedges, to serve

SKORDALIA

4 slices white bread, crusts removed

6 garlic cloves, crushed

salt

⅓ cup blanched almonds, ground

⅔ cup olive oil

freshly squeezed juice of 1 lemon

Make the *skordalia*. Place the bread in a food processor or blender and blend into fine crumbs. Sprinkle in 4 tablespoons of cold water and leave to soak for about 5 minutes. Add the garlic, salt, and ground almonds, and process until smooth and well combined.

With the motor still running, gradually add the olive oil in a continuous stream, until the mixture is thick and smooth. Gradually add the lemon juice in the same way. Turn into a serving bowl, cover, and set aside.

Strip the skin and bones away from the salt cod and discard. Cut the flesh into 2-inch chunks.

Make the batter for the fish. Sift the flour into a large mixing bowl with the salt and freshly ground black pepper. Drizzle the olive oil over the flour and beat in the warm water to make a smooth mixture. Allow to stand at room temperature for about 1 hour.

Beat the egg white in a clean, dry bowl until it holds stiff peaks, then fold into the batter. Heat the oil. Dip the chunks of fish into the batter, then gently place in the hot oil. Cook the fish in batches for 5–7 minutes or until crisp and golden.

Using a slotted spoon, transfer the cooked fritters to a dish lined with absorbent paper towels to drain. Serve the battered fritters with lemon wedges and the *skordalia*.

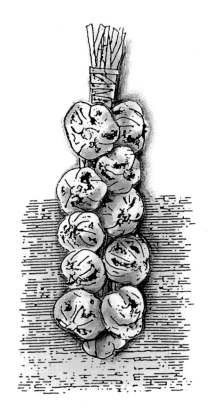

FISH AND VEGETABLE CASSEROLE

SERVES 8 ~ 10

Cod, haddock, or monkfish would all be suitable types of fish to use for this dish, which originates from the
Greek island of Corfu. The crucial ingredient is the garlic, and plenty of it.

INGREDIENTS

6 Tbsp olive oil

1 large onion, sliced

2 lb small new potatoes, washed and cut
into ½-inch slices

2 carrots, cut into 1-inch chunks

1 celery stick, chopped

salt and freshly ground black pepper

6 garlic cloves, crushed

2½ lb firm white fish fillets, skinned and
cut into 2-inch chunks

¼ cup freshly squeezed lemon juice

Heat ¼ cup of the olive oil in a large, heavy saucepan and sauté the onion for about 3 minutes or until softened and slightly brown.

Add the potatoes, carrots, and celery, and season with salt and freshly ground black pepper. Continue to cook for a further 4–5 minutes or until the vegetables begin to soften.

Stir in the garlic and pour over enough boiling water to just cover the vegetables. Bring to a boil, cover, and simmer for 10–15 minutes or until the vegetables are almost tender.

Gently stir the fish into the casserole, cover, and simmer for 10–15 minutes or until the fish flakes easily. Add a little extra water if necessary. Just before the end of the cooking time, remove the cover and stir in the lemon juice and remaining olive oil. Adjust the seasoning if necessary and serve.

MEAT & POULTRY

BEEF AND EGGPLANT BIRIANI

SERVES 6

A wonderful spicy dish for lazy entertaining. Most of it can be prepared in advance and heated through at the last moment. For special occasions, decorate with gold or silver leaf just before serving.

INGREDIENTS

6 Tbsp ghee or sunflower oil

1 lb chuck steak, cut into 1-inch pieces, or
1 lb cooked diced beef

2 bay leaves

2 cups Basmati rice, rinsed

2 large onions, finely sliced

1 tsp curry paste

⅓ cup golden raisins

⅓ cup creamed coconut, finely chopped

CURRY SAUCE

2 onions, roughly chopped

3 garlic cloves, roughly chopped

1 green chile, seeded and chopped

1 Tbsp mild curry paste

2 Tbsp tomato paste

1 Tbsp light brown sugar

⅓ cup ghee or sunflower oil

1 large eggplant, cut into ½-inch dice

1¼ cups light or cereal cream

salt, to taste

2–3 Tbsp chopped fresh cilantro

GARNISHES

2 hard-cooked eggs, quartered

⅓ cup whole blanched almonds,
fried until golden brown

2–3 tomatoes, sliced

Preheat the oven to 325°F. Heat 3 tablespoons of the ghee or oil in a flameproof casserole, brown the steak, then add enough water to cover it over. Add the bay leaves, then bring just to a boil. Cover the casserole and cook in the preheated oven for approximately 2 hours.

Rinse the rice, then bring to a boil in a large pan of cold water. Stir, then cover and cook for 10 minutes. Drain and rinse thoroughly, then drain again.

Prepare the curry sauce. Blend the onions, garlic, and chile with the curry paste, tomato paste, and sugar in a blender or food processor. Heat the ghee or oil in a large skillet, add the eggplant and cook until starting to brown, then add the curry sauce and continue to fry gently for 4–5 minutes. Stir in the cream and bring almost to a gentle simmer, then add salt to taste. Remove from the heat, and set aside, ready to reheat at the last moment.

Heat the remaining ghee or oil in a large skillet or wok, add the onions and cook until golden. Remove half

with a slotted spoon, to use as garnish. Add the curry paste to the onions and cook for a further minute, then add 3 tablespoons of juices from the meat, or water, and cook the mixture for 1 minute longer.

Drain the meat and add it to the pan, or add the left-over cooked meat if using. Stir-fry until it is well heated through and has absorbed the juices. Once hot, add the cooked rice to the pan with the golden raisins and chopped coconut and stir gently until piping hot. Reheat the sauce gently and add the cilantro.

Serve the biriani with the prepared garnishes and with the curry sauce spooned over.

CHICKEN WITH TOMATOES

SERVES 4

You will need lots of saucepans to make this Brazilian dish, but it's well worth

the washing-up at the end!

INGREDIENTS

2 lb roasting chicken, quartered

salt and freshly ground black pepper

3 Tbsp olive oil

4 onions, shredded

5 garlic cloves, crushed

2 x 14-oz cans plum tomatoes, chopped finely

3 Tbsp chopped fresh parsley

1 Tbsp butter

2 Tbsp all-purpose flour

1 cup milk

4 Tbsp grated Parmesan cheese

6 egg whites, beaten to a stiff peak

Put the chicken pieces in a large saucepan, add salt and pepper, and water to cover. Bring to a boil and cook over medium heat for 20 minutes.

Meanwhile, in another saucepan, heat the oil, and fry the onions and garlic for 5 minutes. Add the tomatoes, salt and pepper, and parsley, and cook uncovered for 5 minutes, so that the liquid evaporates.

In a third saucepan, melt the butter, add the flour, and stir well to combine. Add the milk and keep on stirring until the sauce thickens. Turn off the heat and reserve.

When the chicken is cooked, drain, and reserve 1 cup of liquid, skimmed of fat. Discard the rest. Leave the chicken until it is cool enough to handle, then remove the meat from the bones.

Preheat the oven to 375°F. Shred the chicken meat finely and add to the tomato sauce. Then add the white sauce, and check the seasoning.

Transfer the mixture to an ovenproof dish. Scatter the Parmesan cheese over the top. Using a wooden spoon, put peaks of beaten egg whites over it. Bake for 5–10 minutes, or until the whites are cooked and slightly brown. Serve with white rice and deep fried bananas.

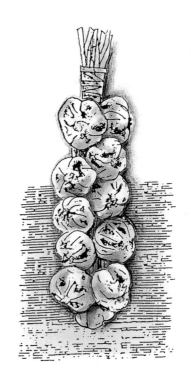

VENISON SAUSAGE AND EGGPLANT CASSEROLE

SERVES 4

Venison sausages have been used for this casserole, but you can use herby or spicy sausages, whichever your prefer.

INGREDIENTS

2 Tbsp olive oil

8 thick venison sausages

2 slices smoked bacon, diced

1 large onion, finely chopped

1 carrot, diced

1–2 garlic cloves, sliced

⅔ cup red wine

1 large eggplant, cut into ½-inch chunks

2 cups canned chopped tomatoes

½ cup French lentils

1 Tbsp tomato paste

1¼ cup beef broth

salt and freshly ground black pepper

parsley sprigs, to garnish

Preheat the oven to 350°F. Heat the oil in a flameproof casserole, then add the sausages and cook them briefly until browned all over. Add the bacon, onion, carrot, and garlic, then cover the casserole and cook slowly for 4–5 minutes.

Add the red wine, then cook rapidly until it is well reduced. Add all the remaining ingredients, then bring to a boil. Cover and cook in the preheated oven for 1 hour.

Season to taste, then garnish with parsley just before serving.

LAMB COOKED IN FOIL

SERVES 8

Authentic Greek kleftiko *is cooked to the point where the meat just falls off the bone. The secret is long, slow cooking in a foil package to allow the flavors to stay trapped inside until the meat is tender.*

INGREDIENTS

8 lamb chops

4 garlic cloves, cut into slivers

¼ cup butter, melted

3 Tbsp freshly squeezed lemon juice

salt and freshly ground black pepper

1 Tbsp dried oregano

1 Tbsp dried mint

Preheat the oven to 350°F. Using a small, sharp knife, make incisions in the chops and insert the slivers of garlic into them. Place each chop in the center of a 12-inch square piece of aluminum foil.

Distribute the remaining ingredients among the 4 chops and gather up the foil, pinching it together at the top to completely encase and seal in the chops and flavorings.

Arrange the foil packages on a cookie sheet and cook for 1½–2 hours, or until the meat is cooked through and very tender. Serve the packages closed, to be opened by each diner.

RABBIT CASSEROLED IN RED WINE

SERVES 6

Rabbit meat is very flavorful but has no fat, so it is ideal in healthy diets.

INGREDIENTS

½ cup butter or lard

1 rabbit, weighing about 4 lb

⅓ cup all-purpose flour

2 garlic cloves, minced

1 large onion, finely minced

2 cups red wine

5 slices lean bacon

20 small onions

1 lb new potatoes

salt and freshly ground black pepper

Preheat the oven to 325°F. Melt half the butter, cut up the rabbit and brown it in the butter for about 5 minutes. Sprinkle the browning pieces with the flour, the crushed garlic, and the finely chopped onion. Add the red wine and enough water to cover the meat. Braise the rabbit, covered, in a warm oven.

While the rabbit is cooking, dice the bacon and peel the small onions. Brown them both in the remaining butter. Set aside.

After 20 minutes, add the bacon and onions to the rabbit. Re-cover.

As the rabbit, bacon, and onions are cooking, peel the new potatoes. After a further 20 minutes, add these to the rabbit.

Cook the casserole for another hour or so, season and serve.

COOK'S TIP
If you cannot find new or baby potatoes, use nicely shaped old ones, carving them a little if you have to.

Rabbit Casseroled in Red Wine ▶

COTTABULLA

SERVES 8

The origins of this old family recipe are obscured in a West Indian mist, but there is nothing vague about Cottabulla itself—a tasty cross between a cold meatloaf and a pâté campagne.

INGREDIENTS

8 oz stale white bread, crusts removed

2 lb ground beef

2 medium onions, finely chopped

2 eggs

1 tsp ground coriander

1 tsp dried oregano

1 Tbsp paprika

3 garlic cloves, crushed

pinch of cayenne

1 tsp sugar

salt and freshly ground black pepper

Preheat the oven to 375°F. Soak the bread in water, squeeze out, and crumble. Mix all the ingredients together thoroughly, seasoning with plenty of salt and pepper.

Pack into a large soufflé dish, leaving a slight hollow in the middle. Cover with foil and bake for 40–50 minutes until cooked through, but still slightly pink in the middle.

While it is still hot, put a plate, slightly smaller than the baking dish, on top of the foil and weight it with some heavy cans. Leave until cold and firm, remove the weights and refrigerate until needed.

Slice into wedges and serve.

COOK'S TIP
This can also be served hot, and there is no need to weight it. Shape into patties, rolled in seasoned flour, to make sensational hamburgers.

MEATBALLS WITH EGGPLANT AND TOMATO SAUCE

SERVES 4

Meatballs make a welcome change to the more usual ground beef sauce for pasta.
Simmer the meatballs gently so that they do not break up during cooking.

INGREDIENTS

1 lb ground lamb

6 scallions, finely chopped

1¼ cups fresh whole wheat bread crumbs

1 Tbsp tomato paste

½ tsp ground turmeric

salt and freshly ground black pepper

1 large egg, beaten

freshly shredded Parmesan cheese, to serve

SAUCE

3 Tbsp olive oil

1 eggplant, cut into ½-inch chunks

1 onion, finely diced

1 garlic clove, finely sliced

½ tsp ground turmeric

1 tsp ground cumin

4 cups canned chopped tomatoes

1 bay leaf

salt and freshly ground black pepper

8–10 fresh basil leaves, torn

Mix all the ingredients for the meatballs together. Shape the mixture with wet hands into walnut-sized balls.

Make the sauce. Heat the oil in a large skillet, then add the eggplant and fry gently until lightly golden. Add the meatballs, together with the onion, garlic, turmeric, and cumin, and cook until the meatballs are browned all over. Add extra oil only if the meatballs are sticking.

Add the tomatoes and bay leaf with salt and pepper and bring the mixture to a boil. Simmer gently for 20 minutes, then season to taste. Add the torn basil leaves to the sauce just before serving.

Serve with pasta, sprinkling a little Parmesan over the meatballs if wished.

BEEF COBBLER

SERVES 6 ~ 8

INGREDIENTS

2 lb stewing steak

½ cup seasoned all-purpose flour

4 Tbsp oil

3 medium onions, cut into 1-inch chunks

4–5 garlic cloves, minced

4–5 large carrots, cut into ½-inch slices

2 tsp dried mixed herbs

1 tsp sugar

1 Tbsp paprika

1 Tbsp tomato paste

1¼ cups red wine

1¼ cups stock or water

SCONE TOPPING

salt and freshly ground black pepper

2¼ cups all-purpose flour

2½ tsp baking powder

4 Tbsp butter or shortening

⅔ cup cold milk and water

Preheat the oven to 400°F. Trim the fat and membrane from the meat and cut the steak into 1¼-inch chunks. Roll the meat in the seasoned flour and fry rapidly in the oil in batches until browned all over. Drain the meat and transfer to a large casserole and sprinkle with any remaining seasoned flour.

Fry the onions and garlic in the remaining oil until they begin to brown and add to the casserole, together with the carrots, herbs, sugar, paprika, tomato paste, wine, stock or water, and plenty of salt and pepper.

Stir gently and cook the uncovered casserole for 20 minutes. Stir after 10 minutes.

Cover the casserole with foil, put its lid on and cook at 325°F for a further 2 hours, stirring from time to time. Add more stock or water if the mixture looks dry.

To make the scone topping, sift together the flour and baking powder and then blend in the butter or shortening until the mixture resembles fine bread crumbs.

Add plenty of salt and pepper to season and enough milk and water to make a soft dough.

Roll out the dough to ½ inch thick on a well-floured surface and stamp out circles 1½–2 inches across.

Taste the stew and adjust the seasoning, adding a little more stock or water if necessary.

Arrange the scone circles on top of the hot stew and cook, uncovered, at 400°F for 20–30 minutes, until the scones are puffy and well browned.

PORK AND RED CHILE BURRITOS

SERVES 4

The pork filling is good not only in burritos, but in tacos, tostadas, tortas, and tamales as well.

INGREDIENTS

2 lb pork shoulder cut
into 1–2 inch cubes

5 ancho chiles

8 garlic cloves, chopped

¼ tsp oregano, crumbled

½ tsp ground cumin

⅓ cup stock

juice of ½ lime

salt and freshly ground black pepper

4 large flour tortillas

simmered pinto beans (see below)

4 Tbsp chopped onion

salsa, to taste

Cover the pork with water and simmer over a low heat for 1 hour or until the water has evaporated and the meat has lightly browned.

Remove the pork from the pan and shred with a fork, tossing it with any juices. Set aside.

Lightly toast the chiles, then remove the stems, seeds, and veins. Break or cut them up into small pieces, then place in a saucepan with boiling water to cover. Simmer for 15–20 minutes or until they plump up.

In a blender or food processor, combine the chiles, garlic, oregano, cumin, stock, and lime juice until they form a smooth paste.

Heat the meat in its juices and pan drippings, then add the sauce and mix well. Simmer over a low heat for about 20 minutes or until the meat has absorbed the chili sauce. Season with salt and pepper, and adjust the cumin and oregano to taste.

Warm the tortillas. Into each one, spoon a generous portion of meat, a ladle of beans, then a sprinkling of onion, and salsa to taste. Roll up tightly and serve right away, while still hot.

SIMMERED BEANS

SERVES 6 ~ 8

Use these beans as an accompaniment to make frijoles refritos, *or anywhere it calls for simmered beans. A bowl of warm* frijoles de olla, *along with a few warm tortillas and a chile or two is the mainstay of the Mexican diet.*

INGREDIENTS

1 lb pinto (or pinquito, or pink) or black beans, picked over for stones etc, soaked

2 medium onions, chopped

1 head of garlic, unpeeled and cut into halves crosswise

8 oz smoky bacon

several sprigs of mint

salt

Soak the beans in a bowl overnight. Alternatively, place the beans in a saucepan with enough cold water to cover. Bring to a boil, cook for a few minutes, then remove from the heat. Leave, covered, for 1 hour. The beans should have plumped up and softened somewhat, as they will have absorbed the water in the process.

Add the onion, garlic, bacon, mint, and water to the pan.

Bring to a boil, then reduce the heat to low and simmer, uncovered, stirring once or twice, for 1½–2 hours or until the beans are softened. Add salt to taste.

SPICED PORK AND EGGPLANT CHOP SUEY

SERVES 4

A spiced, Chinese-style dish of marinated pork and crispy, stir-fried vegetables. Make up your own vegetable mix, or use prepared stir-fry vegetables from the market if you are in a hurry. Serve with boiled rice or thread egg noodles.

INGREDIENTS

1 pork tenderloin, weighing about 1 lb

1½ lb mixed stir-fry vegetables, such as celery, carrot, bell peppers, snow peas, beansprouts

1 eggplant, halved lengthwise and sliced thinly

4 Tbsp peanut oil

MARINADE

2-inch piece fresh ginger, roughly minced

1–2 garlic cloves, minced

1 Tbsp five-spice powder

1 green chile, deseeded and very finely chopped

4 Tbsp soy sauce

1 Tbsp chili sauce

1 Tbsp light brown sugar

Trim the pork and cut it into very thin slices. Squeeze the juice from the minced ginger and mix it with the other marinade ingredients, then add the pork and toss the slices in the mixture. Leave to stand for at least 1 hour, turning occasionally.

Meanwhile, prepare the vegetables for the stir-fry, cutting them all into thin 2-inch lengths.

Heat the oil in a wok or large skillet until almost smoking, then add the pork and the eggplant. Stir-fry for

about 4 minutes until both are well browned, then add the remaining vegetables. Continue to cook for a further 2–3 minutes, adding any remaining marinade. Serve the pork dish immediately.

SAUTÉED LAMB WITH EGGPLANT IN A SAUCE

SERVES 4

INGREDIENTS

2 large eggplants, ends cut off and
thickly sliced

3 Tbsp olive oil

8 lamb cutlets, trimmed

2 garlic cloves, minced

6 large tomatoes, blanched, skinned, and
thickly sliced

salt and freshly ground black pepper

1 lemon, sliced, to garnish

sprigs of mint, to garnish

SAUCE

2 Tbsp chopped fresh mint

⅔ cup natural unsweetened yogurt

freshly ground black pepper

Sprinkle salt over the sliced eggplant and leave for 20 minutes. Rinse the slices and dry with absorbent paper towels.

Heat 2 tablespoons of olive oil in a wok or large skillet over a very high heat and add the lamb cutlets. When the meat is brown, lower the heat and continue to cook until the meat is tender, which will take about 5 minutes on each side. Remove the cutlets from the wok, drain on absorbent paper towels, and keep warm in the oven.

Add the remaining oil to the wok and fry the eggplant slices with the garlic until they are lightly browned on both sides. If the oil dries out, add a little more. When the eggplant is cooked, push the slices up the sides of the wok and add the tomato slices. Stir-fry for a few moments and season with salt and pepper.

Make the sauce. Stir the mint into the yogurt and grind over some black pepper. Serve in a small bowl.

Place the vegetables on a dish and arrange the cutlets over them. Serve garnished with lemon slices and sprigs of fresh mint.

SHEPHERD'S PIE

SERVES 6

This dish makes a filling supper and is great for feeding lots of
hungry people.

INGREDIENTS

1½ lb potatoes

2 medium onions, finely minced

2 garlic cloves, minced

3 Tbsp olive oil

2 Tbsp tomato paste

⅔ cup red wine

1 tsp oregano or 2 tsp fresh
majoram, chopped

1 tsp dried basil or 2 tsp finely
chopped fresh basil

2 tsp paprika

1 tsp sugar

salt and freshly ground black pepper

1½ lb ground beef

4 Tbsp butter

2 Tbsp light or cereal cream

1 Tbsp Parmesan cheese or
2 Tbsp Cheddar cheese

Preheat the oven to 400°F. Peel the potatoes and cut into 1-inch chunks. Boil them in plenty of salted water for 15 minutes, until tender.

Meanwhile, soften the onions and garlic in the olive oil over a low heat, then turn up the heat and add the tomato paste, wine, herbs, paprika, and sugar, and season with salt and pepper.

Add the beef and cook over a moderate heat for about 10 minutes, stirring from time to time, until the meat loses its pinkness.

Drain the potatoes, season with plenty of salt and pepper, and mash well, adding first the butter and then the cream.

Spread the warm beef in a baking dish and cover completely with the mashed potato.

Sprinkle with the cheese and bake for 20–30 minutes, depending on the thickness of the meat and potato.

Brown the top under a hot broiler.

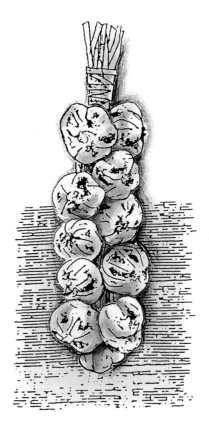

ROSEMARY-ROASTED PORK WITH BRAISED MUSHROOMS

SERVES 6

Braised mushrooms, Catalan-style, added to the pan juices make a luscious sauce for roasted meat.

Most mushrooms are delicious, but you must use fresh tomatoes—canned won't do.

INGREDIENTS

2½ lb boned, lean pork, roasted (rolled, by the butcher, and tied, is excellent and will help it stay tidy during roasting)

several sprigs fresh rosemary

10–12 garlic cloves, half cut into slivers, half chopped

salt and freshly ground black pepper

4 Tbsp olive oil

2 carrots, diced

10 garlic cloves, left whole but peeled

1 large onion, chopped

3 fresh ripe tomatoes, shredded and skins discarded

1 lb mixed fresh wild mushrooms, or cultivated common mushrooms mixed with a few handfuls of dried mixed exotic mushrooms

dry white wine or stock, if needed

Preheat the oven to 350°F. Make incisions all over the meat. Into each one insert a sprig of rosemary, which you have dipped into a little salt, and a sliver of garlic. Stud the whole roast, then rub it with olive oil.

Scatter the carrots, whole garlic cloves, and a few rosemary sprigs on the base of a roasting pan. Place the roast on a roasting rack, if you have one, or on the base of the pan. Place in the oven for 1¼ hours.

Meanwhile, sauté the onion slowly in the remaining olive oil, sprinkling with salt to draw out the juices, until soft, which takes about 20 minutes. Stir in the chopped garlic, then add the tomatoes and raise the heat, cooking until the tomatoes melt into the onions, and the oil begins to separate.

Add the mushrooms, reduce the heat, and cook over medium–low heat, stirring occasionally, until the mushrooms are cooked through. The moisture from the fresh mushrooms should rehydrate any dried ones used, but if they don't, add a little stock or dry white wine to the pan, and boil until the mushrooms rehydrate.

When the mushrooms are tender, season with salt and pepper, and set aside until the meat is ready. (A meat thermometer is useful here so that you can gauge the inside of the meat without cutting into it.)

Remove the cooked pork from its pan, pour off any fat from the surface but save any juices, then add a few tablespoons of wine or stock. Place on the stove and scrape the base of the pan. Add the braised mushrooms and warm through, then set aside and keep warm.

Slice the roast, and serve each portion with a few spoonfuls of the mushroom sauce.

SHEPHERD'S BUSH CASSOULET

SERVES 6 ~ 8

The ingredients in this casserole make it into a more interesting variation
of this classic method of cooking. As you can prepare it well in advance,
it is ideal for feeding large numbers of people.

INGREDIENTS

1 lb white navy beans

8 oz piece raw, unsalted bacon

1 bay leaf

8 oz Toulouse or Polish sausage,
cut into 1-inch chunks

2 lb boned shoulder or breast of lamb
cut into 1½-inch chunks

seasoned all-purpose flour

3 Tbsp olive oil

2 medium onions, sliced

4 garlic cloves, minced

2 Tbsp tomato paste

1 tsp sugar

½ tsp dried thyme

½ tsp dried oregano

1¼ cups red wine

salt and freshly ground black pepper

2 cups stock or water

Preheat the oven to 400°F. Wash the navy beans and soak them in cold water overnight.

Change the water, add the bacon and the bay leaf and simmer, covered, for an hour. Drain, discard the bay leaf and cut the bacon into 1-inch chunks. Put the bacon, beans, and Toulouse or Polish sausage into a large casserole.

Roll the meat in seasoned flour and brown in oil. Transfer to the casserole.

Fry the onions and garlic in the remains of the oil until they begin to brown. Add the tomato paste, sugar, herbs, wine, and plenty of salt and pepper. Simmer for a couple of minutes, then pour into the casserole, together with the stock or water.

Put the casserole, uncovered, into a hot oven for 20 minutes, stirring gently from time to time. Cover the casserole, turn down the heat to 325°F and cook for a further 2½ hours, stirring occasionally, until the lamb and beans are tender.

You may need to add a little more water, if the casserole looks as if it is getting dry.

FRESH CHICKEN WITH LEMON GRASS AND CASHEW NUTS

SERVES 4

This delicious main course is surprisingly quick and easy.

Serve with a bowl of steaming rice.

INGREDIENTS

vegetable oil

2 small dried chiles

1 garlic clove, chopped

1 lb lean, corn-fed chicken, sliced

½ tsp sugar

1 Tbsp oyster sauce

1 Tbsp Nuoc Mam sauce or
light soy sauce

3 Tbsp chicken stock or water

½ cup roasted, unsalted cashew nuts

1 Tbsp chopped lemon grass

2 shallots, cut in quarters

With a drop or two of oil, stir-fry the chiles until cooked evenly but not burnt. Set aside.

Stir-fry the garlic with a few more drops of oil until golden. Add the chicken slices, sugar, and oyster and Nuoc Mam sauces, and stir-fry until the chicken is golden in color. Lower the heat and add the stock. Cook for a few more minutes, stirring occasionally.

When the chicken is thoroughly cooked, add the cashew nuts, lemon grass, shallots, and chiles, and stir several times, being careful not to break the chiles. Remove from the heat and serve.

COLD CHICKEN MILLEFOGLIE

SERVES 4 ~ 6

This cold dish is great for summer parties outdoors. Serve with a selection of your favorite salads and crusty white bread.

INGREDIENTS

12 oz puff pastry

½ cup Basic Garlic Dressing (page 180)

8–10 canned artichoke hearts, quartered

½ Tbsp oil

1 garlic clove, minced

1 tsp ground coriander

½ tsp ground cumin

½ tsp turmeric

½ tsp paprika

2 pinches cayenne pepper

1 Tbsp lemon juice

1 cup stiffly whipped cream

8 oz cold cooked chicken, cut or torn into bite-sized pieces

salt and freshly ground black pepper

2 Tbsp finely chopped parsley

1 Tbsp mayonnaise or Aïoli (page 171)

Preheat the oven to 450°F. Roll the pastry out thinly and cut into 3 strips, approximately 4 inches wide. Prick all over with a fork and bake for 7–10 minutes until well risen and browned. Cool on wire rack until needed. Warm the Basic Garlic Dressing and pour over the artichoke hearts. Set aside for at least 1 hour.

Make the sauce for the chicken. Heat the oil and add to it the garlic, coriander, cumin, turmeric, paprika, and cayenne. Stir over a moderate heat for several minutes. Remove from the heat and add the lemon juice, and either pour or strain the mixture into the cream. Fold the chicken into the sauce and season with salt and pepper to taste.

To assemble the Millefoglie, put one slice of cooked pastry on a serving dish and spread over it half the chicken mixture. Drain the dressing from the artichoke hearts, mix into them the parsley and put half of this on top of the chicken. Top with the second piece of pastry, the remaining chicken, and the rest of the artichoke mixture.

Spread the underside of the final pastry slice with the mayonnaise or Aïoli and press it gently, sticky side down, onto the artichoke and parsley mixture.

Slice with a very sharp serrated knife and serve immediately.

CHICKEN MOUSSAKA

SERVES 4 ~ 6

*Moussaka is one of the classic eggplant dishes, and this is one of the best
moussaka recipes ever. Use a covered pan to start the sauce as less oil
is required if the onion is half steamed in its own juices.*

INGREDIENTS

½ cup olive oil

2 large onions, chopped

1 lb boneless chicken, finely diced or
chopped in the food processor

1–2 garlic cloves, minced

⅔ cup red wine

2 cups canned chopped tomatoes

2 Tbsp freshly chopped oregano, plus
extra for garnish

salt and freshly ground black pepper

1 Tbsp tomato paste

2 large eggplants, sliced

butter, for greasing

TOPPING

1 cup ricotta cheese

½ cup soft goat's cheese with
garlic and herbs

⅔ cup unsweetened yogurt

Heat 2 tablespoons of the oil in a pan, add the onions, cover and cook gently until soft. Remove the lid and stir in the chicken with the garlic. Cook quickly until the chicken changes color. Add the wine and cook until it has reduced by half. Add all the other ingredients except the eggplants, then simmer slowly for 30–40 minutes, until rich and thick.

Preheat the oven to 425°F. Add 3–4 tablespoons of the oil to a skillet. Fry the eggplant slices a few at a time until browned on both sides, adding more oil as necessary. Remove with a slotted spoon and drain the slices on paper towels.

Layer the chicken sauce and eggplant slices in a buttered, oven-proof dish, finishing with a layer of eggplant. Make the topping. Blend the cheeses and yogurt together into a sauce, add salt and pepper to taste, and spoon the mixture over the eggplant. Bake for 25–30 minutes. Serve the chicken sprinkled with chopped oregano.

RED DUCK CURRY

SERVES 6

This is a very popular dish in Thailand; rich and quite delicious.

INGREDIENTS

7 cups thin coconut milk

1 roasted duck, boned with skin left on, cut into ½-inch slices

15 cherry tomatoes

5 fresh large red chiles, sliced lengthwise

1 cup/2½ oz sweet basil leaves

3 kaffir lime leaves, chopped

3 Tbsp sugar

2 Tbsp fish sauce

1 tsp salt

RED CURRY PASTE

3 stalks of lemon grass, sliced thinly

1½ oz chopped galangal (ka)

7 dried red chiles, chopped roughly

3 Tbsp chopped garlic

1 Tbsp shrimp paste

1 tsp chopped kaffir lime leaf

1 tsp chopped coriander root

1 tsp white peppercorns

½ tsp coriander seeds

Pound all the curry paste ingredients together with a mortar and pestle or in a blender to a fine paste.

Heat 2 cups of the coconut milk in a wok or pan, add the curry paste mixture, and cook together for 5 minutes. Add the rest of the coconut milk, bring to a boil, then add the duck, cherry tomatoes, and red chile. Bring back to a boil and then add the rest of the ingredients.

Boil all together for 5 minutes and remove from the heat.

Serve accompanied with rice, salted eggs, and sun-dried beef.

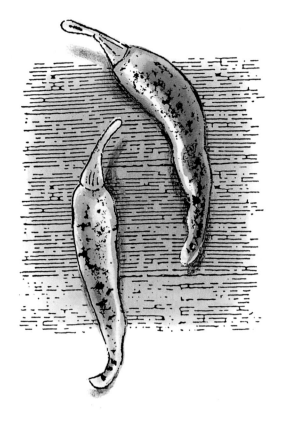

CHICKEN CREOLE

SERVES 6 ~ 8

This is also a good way of cooking cod steaks—there is no need to fry them first.

INGREDIENTS

8 chicken portions

4 oz peeled shrimp

2 Tbsp olive oil

½ tsp dried tarragon

2 garlic cloves, minced

¼ tsp hot pepper sauce or cayenne

1 large onion, thinly sliced

1 red bell pepper, cored and thinly sliced

Concentrated Tomato Sauce (page 181)

Preheat the oven to 350°F. Score the chicken pieces and put them in a dish, with the shrimp at one end. Pour over them a mixture of the oil, tarragon, garlic, and hot pepper sauce or cayenne. Leave to marinate for at least 1 hour before cooking.

Drain the marinade into a skillet and remove the shrimp, keeping to one side until needed.

Fry the chicken in the heated marinade for 7–10 minutes, turning occasionally, until well browned.

Arrange in a roasting pan.

Fry the onion and bell pepper in the oil left in the skillet until the onion begins to brown, then arrange over the chicken.

Pour the tomato sauce over the vegetables and chicken, cover the pan with foil, and cook for 30 minutes. Remove the foil, increase the heat to 425°F, and bake for another 20 minutes, adding the shrimp 5 minutes before serving, to heat them through.

GARLIC CHICKEN ON A STICK

SERVES 6

Soak wooden skewers in lemon juice for about 30 minutes before use to stop them from burning.

INGREDIENTS

6 chicken breast halves, skinned and boned

6 garlic cloves, minced

salt and freshly ground black pepper

freshly squeezed juice of 2 lemons

¼ cup olive oil

6 Tbsp finely chopped fresh parsley

Cut the chicken halves into 1-inch pieces and place them in a shallow dish.

In a small bowl, mix together the garlic, salt and freshly ground pepper, lemon juice, and olive oil. Pour the marinade over the chicken, stir to coat the meat, cover the dish, and place in the refrigerator for 2–4 hours, turning the chicken and rearranging the pieces from time to time.

Spread the chopped parsley on a serving plate.

Divide the chicken pieces into 6 equal portions, reserving the marinade, and thread the meat on to 6 wooden skewers. Roll each skewer in the chopped parsley to coat evenly.

Arrange the chicken skewers on an oiled broiler rack and cook under a preheated broiler for 5–10 minutes or until the chicken is golden on the outside and cooked through. Turn and rearrange the skewers, basting with the reserved marinade to add flavor while the meat cooks.

THANKSGIVING MOLE

SERVES 8

This streamlined version of one of Mexico's most famous national dishes makes a change from the usual methods of dealing with the remains of the Christmas or Thanksgiving turkey and is equally good made with chicken. Serve it with plain boiled rice, refried beans, tortillas, and a bowl of Guacamole.

INGREDIENTS

turkey bones

5 cups water

2 medium onions, coarsely chopped

4 garlic cloves, coarsely chopped

salt and freshly ground black pepper

4 oz canned pimentos, coarsely chopped

1 small red bell pepper, deseeded and chopped

¾ cup/12 oz ripe tomatoes, skinned, deseeded and chopped

1 thick slice of white bread, toasted and crumbled

1 cup ground almonds

⅓ cup sesame seeds

2 Tbsp oil or lard

1 tsp ground coriander

½ tsp ground allspice

chili powder, to taste

2 tsp brown sugar

¼ cup unsweetened chocolate, in small pieces

2 lb cold turkey meat, torn into bite-sized pieces

Gently simmer the turkey bones in the water with a third of the onion, a quarter of the garlic, and plenty of salt and pepper for 45 minutes, by which time you should have a good stock.

Combine the remaining onion and garlic, pimentos, red bell pepper, tomatoes, bread, ground almonds, half the sesame seeds, and half the turkey stock, and reduce to a smooth purée.

In a large, heavy saucepan, heat the oil or lard, coriander, allspice, chili powder—you can always add more later if it's not hot enough for you— and sugar, for a couple of minutes.

Add the puréed sauce and stir over a moderate heat for 5 minutes. Add the chocolate and enough stock to dilute the sauce to the thickness of heavy cream. Season with salt and pepper to taste.

Turn down the heat and cook gently, stirring occasionally, for 10 minutes. Add the turkey and heat for a further 10 minutes.

Toss the remaining sesame seeds over a moderate heat until toasted and sprinkle them over the turkey just before serving.

Korean Braised Chicken Thighs ▶

KOREAN BRAISED CHICKEN THIGHS

SERVES 4

Chicken thighs become richly flavored and very tender and succulent when they are steeped
in a tasty marinade, then fried and braised in it.

INGREDIENTS

8 chicken thighs

4 scallions, white parts only, very
finely chopped

1-inch piece of fresh ginger, grated

2 garlic cloves, minced

4 Tbsp soy sauce

1 Tbsp sesame oil

1½ Tbsp crushed toasted sesame seeds

2 tsp sugar

vegetable oil for frying

1 red bell pepper, seeded and diced

2 scallions, white and pale green parts,
sliced diagonally

Slash each chicken thigh three times and place them in a shallow dish. Mix together the finely chopped scallions, the ginger, garlic, soy sauce, sesame oil, sesame seeds, and sugar. Pour over the chicken. Turn to coat with the sauce and leave in a cool place for about 4 hours, turning occasionally.

Heat a little vegetable oil in a heavy flameproof casserole. Lift the chicken thighs from the marinade, add to the casserole, brown evenly. Pour in the marinade and enough water just to cover the chicken. Bring barely to simmering point. Cover the casserole and leave to cook gently for about 30–35 minutes, turning the chicken occasionally, until very tender.

Add the red bell pepper and sliced scallions about 5 minutes before the end of cooking. If necessary, uncover the casserole toward the end of cooking to let the sauce reduce.

LIVER STROGANOFF

SERVES 4

INGREDIENTS

1 lb calves' liver, thinly sliced

1 garlic clove, minced and the juice

1 Tbsp oil

½ tsp fresh bruised sage leaves, chopped

6 black peppercorns, bruised

½ tsp paprika

2 Tbsp dry white wine or dry sherry

2 cups/8 oz baby onions

4 Tbsp butter

4 Tbsp all-purpose flour

⅔ cup sour cream

salt and freshly ground black pepper

Cut the liver into strips ¼ x 2 inch. Pour over them a mixture of the minced garlic, oil, sage, peppercorns, paprika, and wine or sherry, and leave to marinate in a cool place for 2–4 hours, stirring occasionally.

Peel the onions—this is easier if you first loosen the skins by blanching them in boiling water for 30 seconds—and sweat them in the butter, covered, for 10–20 minutes, until they are just tender. Remove the onions from the pan and reserve.

Drain the liver of its marinade, toss it in the flour, and cook in the butter and onion juices for no more than a minute on each side.

Add the garlic juice and onions, and simmer for a minute more. Off the heat, stir in the sour cream, season with salt and pepper to taste, and serve immediately.

DOUBLE GARLIC CHICKEN

SERVES 4 ~ 6

Definitely a dish for garlic lovers. The chicken is flavored both

inside and out for a full garlic experience.

INGREDIENTS

3 heads garlic (about 35 cloves)

3½–4 lb roasting chicken

¾ cup cream cheese or
low-fat soft cheese

1 Tbsp chopped chives

1 Tbsp chopped parsley

salt and freshly ground black pepper

8 oz green grapes
(seedless and not too sweet)

sprig of rosemary

2 Tbsp butter

Preheat the oven to 350°F. Plunge the unpeeled garlic, except for 2 cloves, into a pan of boiling water for 30 seconds, drain, and peel.

Boil for a further 2 minutes, drain, and set to one side.

Peel one of the remaining garlic cloves, and cut it in half. Rub the cut side of the garlic over the breast and legs of the chicken, then slice it and its other half.

Peel and crush the last garlic clove and blend it with the cream or low-fat cheese, chives, and parsley. Season well with salt and pepper.

Work your fingers under the skin of the chicken breast, carefully freeing it from the meat without tearing it.

Pack the cheese mixture between the loosened skin and the meat, covering the breast completely.

Stuff the body of the chicken with the blanched garlic and the grapes, together with most of the rosemary.

Put the chicken in an oiled roasting pan and tuck slices of garlic and the remaining blades of rosemary between the legs and wings and the body of the chicken.

Sprinkle the breast with salt and dot it with the butter. Cover the breast and feet with foil.

Bake for approximately 1½ hours, until the juice no longer runs pink, removing the foil for the last 20 minutes of cooking to crisp the skin.

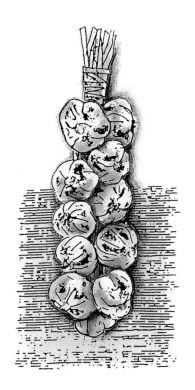

CHICKEN WINGS WITH LIME JUICE AND GARLIC

SERVES 8 ~ 12

Whenever you buy a whole chicken, freeze the wings if they are not needed. When you have enough collected in the freezer, you can transform them into this deliciously tangy recipe.

INGREDIENTS

12 chicken wings

4 garlic cloves, minced

salt and freshly ground black pepper

freshly squeezed juice of 4 limes

pinch of cayenne pepper

Place the chicken wings in a shallow dish. Rub the minced garlic all over the chicken wings, then season them with salt and freshly ground black pepper.

Sprinkle the lime juice and cayenne pepper over the chicken wings, cover, and marinate in the refrigerator for 3–4 hours, turning and rearranging them occasionally.

Arrange the chicken wings in a large skillet and pour the marinade over them. Add just enough cold water to cover the wings and bring quickly to a boil. Cook, uncovered, for 20–25 minutes, or until the chicken is cooked through and the sauce has reduced slightly. Serve warm or, better still, cold the next day.

CHICKEN WITH PRUNES

SERVES 4

Prunes make a rich, winey sauce, their sweetness balanced with the spicy, smoky chile and the tangy edge of tamarind. Serve with boiled potatoes sprinkled with cumin and green onions, or with steamed rice tossed with strips of roasted peeled green peppers and sautéed onions, with a sprinkling of cumin.

INGREDIENTS

1 chicken, cut into serving pieces

juice of ½ lime or 4–6 crushed cooked tomatillos

5 garlic cloves, chopped

chipotle salsa or marinade from chipotle chiles, to taste

salt and freshly ground black pepper

flour for dusting

vegetable oil

6–8 tomatoes, diced

1 onion, chopped

½ cup wine, beer or brandy

1½ cups chicken stock

10–12 prunes, pitted

2–3 Tbsp sugar or honey

1 Tbsp tamarind paste or Worcestershire sauce, to taste

½ tsp ground cinnamon

¼ tsp ground allspice or large dash of ground cloves

vinegar

2 Tbsp lightly toasted slivered almonds, to garnish

1 Tbsp chopped fresh cilantro, to garnish

Combine the chicken with the lime juice or tomatillos, half the garlic, the chipotle salsa, and salt and pepper. Leave to marinate for 1 hour or better still overnight.

Dust the chicken with flour then lightly brown in oil in a skillet, taking care it does not burn. Place in a casserole, then pour out the fat from the skillet.

Add the tomatoes, onion, wine, beer or brandy, chicken stock, and remaining garlic to the skillet, and bring to a boil. Simmer for a few minutes until the onion turns translucent, then add the prunes, sugar or honey, tamarind paste or Worcestershire sauce, cinnamon, cloves, and chipotle to taste.

Pour the sauce into the casserole, letting it lightly coat the chicken and sink to the bottom of the casserole. Place the prunes under the chicken.

Bake the chicken in a preheated oven at 350°F for 35–45 minutes or until very tender. Adjust seasoning and serve, sprinkled with toasted almonds and cilantro.

MOROCCAN CHICKEN WITH LEMONS AND OLIVES

SERVES 4

There is little work involved in preparing this dish, which basically simmers away in the oven, and it is never less than delicious.

INGREDIENTS

1 chicken, cut into serving pieces

1 Tbsp cumin

2 tsp paprika

½–1 tsp ginger

½–1 tsp turmeric

5 garlic cloves, chopped

several handfuls of fresh cilantro, chopped

juice of 2 lemons

black and cayenne pepper, to taste

3–5 Tbsp all-purpose flour

4 tomatoes, chopped
(either ripe or canned)

10–15 each (three types in total): green
olives of choice, black olives, cracked
olives, oil-cured olives, purplish-red olives,
Kalamata, pimiento-stuffed green olives,
etc., drained

¼ cup extra-virgin olive oil

1 cup chicken broth

1 lemon, cut into 6 wedges

extra lemon juice, to taste

Preheat the oven to 325°F. Combine the chicken with the cumin, paprika, ginger, turmeric, garlic, cilantro, lemon juice, and pepper, and place in a baking dish in a single layer. Leave to marinate for 30 minutes, then add the flour, and toss together to coat well.

Add the tomatoes, olives, lemon wedges, olive oil, and broth to the dish. Bake uncovered for about 1 hour, or until the chicken is tender and a delicious sauce has formed.

VEGETABLES & SALADS

SAVORY ROASTED PUMPKIN

SERVES 4

Drizzling the pumpkin or squash with olive oil and balsamic vinegar, then baking it,
is a simple, healthy way to serve this rich, sweet vegetable.

INGREDIENTS

2½ lb pumpkin, or large orange squash
or other winter squash, cut
into several pieces

3–5 garlic cloves, chopped

3 Tbsp extra-virgin olive oil

I tsp balsamic vinegar

sea salt and freshly ground black pepper

pinch of mild, red chili powder

pinch of oregano or sage

Arrange the squash or pumpkin on a baking sheet, and sprinkle all of the other ingredients over it.

Cover tightly with foil, and bake for about an hour at 350°F, or until the pumpkin or squash is tender. Unwrap and serve hot.

COOK'S TIP

If you have any left-overs these may be mashed with a fork, smoothed with a bit of extra-virgin olive oil, a little chopped garlic, a few drops of lemon, and served as a Mediterranean antipasto or meze-type salad.

POTATO AND TOMATO GRATIN

SERVES 4 ~ 6

This gratin layers potatoes with tomatoes and olive-oil-cooked onions, unlike many other gratins,
which are creamy and cheesy. This is terrific warm, but like many dishes cooked in olive oil,
it is best served at room temperature the next day.

INGREDIENTS

2½ lb potatoes, preferably waxy ones,
peeled and cut into halves

3–4 onions, thinly sliced

¼ cup extra-virgin olive oil

8 garlic cloves, chopped

salt and freshly ground black pepper

2 cups tomatoes (canned are fine),
coarsely diced or broken up

I Tbsp chopped fresh oregano

Parboil the potatoes for about 15 minutes, until they are nearly cooked. Remove from the water and leave to cool for about 15 minutes, or until you are able to handle them. Then peel and cut into ⅛-inch thick slices.

Meanwhile, sauté the onions in a few tablespoons of olive oil, and when they have softened, sprinkle in half the garlic. Season with salt and pepper, and continue to cook until softened and lightly browned.

Layer the onions in the bottom of a 14-inch casserole dish, then layer the sliced potatoes and tomatoes, with the remaining garlic, olive oil, salt, and pepper, ending with a layer of the tomatoes and a drizzle of olive oil.

Sprinkle with oregano, then bake in a 375–400°F oven for 20–30 minutes, or until the top is lightly browned, the whole thing is sizzling, and the potatoes have cooked through.

Savory Roasted Pumpkin ▶

GARLIC MASH

SERVES 6

This is particularly good with sausages, steak, and roast chicken, or as a nest for baked eggs.
Don't count on left-overs, but if there are any they can be chilled, shaped into patties,
rolled in flour, and shallow fried in hot fat until brown on both sides.

INGREDIENTS

3 heads garlic (about 35 cloves)

½ cup butter

2 Tbsp all-purpose flour

¼ tsp nutmeg

¼ tsp English mustard

1¼ cups boiling milk

salt and freshly ground black pepper

8 cups/2 lb floury potatoes

3 Tbsp light or cereal cream

Separate the garlic cloves and blanch them in boiling water for 1 minute, drain and peel.

Cook them over a low heat, covered, in half the butter for about 20 minutes until tender.

Blend in the flour, nutmeg, and mustard, and stir for several minutes without browning.

Remove from the heat and stir in the boiling milk. Season with plenty of salt and pepper.

Return to the pan and simmer for 2 more minutes.

Peel the potatoes and cut into small chunks. Boil for 15 minutes or until just tender and drain. Mash with the remaining butter.

Beat in the reheated garlic purée followed by the cream, one spoonful at a time. The final mixture should not be too runny. Season the mash with salt and pepper to taste and serve immediately.

OIL-ROASTED ROOT VEGETABLES

SERVES 4

Root vegetables are delicious when cut into chunks or chips and drenched in olive oil before
being roasted to a crispy-brown exterior and a tender, creamy inside.

INGREDIENTS

2 of each: carrots, parsnips, potatoes, turnips, celery root, sweet potatoes, or any root vegetable you can find

2–3 Tbsp extra-virgin olive oil

salt and freshly ground black pepper

2–3 garlic cloves, chopped

Cut the vegetables into chunks or chips, and blanch them quickly. Drain and toss them in olive oil, salt, and pepper, and then arrange on a baking sheet.

Preheat the oven to 400°F. Roast the vegetables until they are browned and crisp, turning every so soften. Toss them with garlic, and serve.

CHESTNUT HASH

SERVES 4

Cook the potatoes for this dish in advance or use up any left-over cooked potatoes for speed.

Allow the potato to brown on the base of the pan for a crunchier texture.

INGREDIENTS

1½ lb potatoes, peeled and cubed

1 red onion, halved and sliced

½ cup snow peas

½ cup broccoli flowerets

1 zucchini, sliced

1 green bell pepper, deseeded and sliced

¼ cup drained, canned corn

2 garlic cloves, chopped

1 tsp paprika

2 Tbsp chopped fresh parsley

1¼ cups vegetable oil

⅓ cup chestnuts, cooked, peeled, and quartered

freshly ground black pepper

parsley sprigs, to garnish

Cook the potatoes in boiling water for 20 minutes or until softened. Drain well and reserve.

Meanwhile, cook the remaining ingredients in a skillet for 10 minutes, stirring. Add the drained potatoes to the skillet and cook for a further 15 minutes, stirring and pressing down with the back of a spoon. Serve immediately with crusty bread.

BUTTER-BRAISED GARLIC

SERVES 3 ~ 4

Garlic was popular as a vegetable during the Middle Ages, when it was known as "aquapatys."
It is certainly time that this surprisingly subtle dish had a revival.

INGREDIENTS

4 good-sized heads of garlic
(about 60 cloves)

6 Tbsp butter

salt and freshly ground black pepper

2 Tbsp finely chopped fresh
parsley, to serve

Separate the garlic cloves and simmer in salted water for 15 minutes, until just tender.

Drain, peel carefully and stew them in the butter over a low heat for a further 5–7 minutes. Season with salt and pepper.

Stir in the chopped parsley and serve the hot garlic.

EGGPLANT AND SWEET POTATO CURRY

SERVES 4

This makes a very substantial main course, but it could also be served as a side dish
with meat or fish curries.

INGREDIENTS

2 tsp cumin seeds

1 Tbsp mustard seeds

3 Tbsp ghee or sunflower oil

2 small sweet potatoes, about 1 lb, peeled
and cut into ½-inch chunks

1 large onion, finely sliced

2 garlic cloves, finely sliced

1–2 tsp chili powder

1 tsp ground turmeric

1 large eggplant, cut the same
size as the potato

1 Tbsp blue poppy seeds

1 cup water or vegetable broth

2 tsp salt

1 Tbsp torn fresh cilantro leaves

Heat a large skillet over a medium heat, then add the cumin and mustard seeds and dry-fry for 30 seconds or so, until they are aromatic and starting to pop. Transfer to a plate and leave to cool.

Heat the ghee or oil in the pan, add the potatoes and cook for 3–4 minutes until starting to soften. Add the onion, garlic, chili powder, and turmeric and cook for 1–2 minutes, then add the eggplant with the roasted spices and the poppy seeds. Stir in the water or broth and salt, then cover and simmer very slowly for 30–45 minutes until the vegetables are tender.

Season the curry to taste, then serve sprinkled with the cilantro.

Eggplant and Sweet Potato Curry ▶

GRATIN OF POTATOES AND MUSHROOMS

SERVES 4

Soaking the potatoes makes a lighter, less stodgy gratin. If you have no trompettes de la mort,
use porcini, morels, or a combination of mixed dried mushrooms.

INGREDIENTS

2 oz trompettes de la mort

1 cup stock or water

8 baking potatoes (about 2½ lb in total)

salt and freshly ground black pepper

10 shallots, chopped or sliced

8–10 garlic cloves, chopped

½ cup butter

1½ cups light cream

2 cups shredded Parmesan, comte, fontina,
or Gruyère cheese, or a
combination, for sprinkling

1 Tbsp pink peppercorns

2 Tbsp chopped fresh parsley

Place the mushrooms in a saucepan with the stock or water and bring to a boil. Reduce the heat, simmer for 5–10 minutes, or until the mushrooms are tender, then remove them from the heat.

When the mushrooms are cool enough to handle, remove them from the saucepan, and set aside. Strain the mushroom liquid and set aside.

Peel and thinly slice the potatoes, and place them in cold water to cover. Leave for about 30 minutes, then drain, and dry well. Use a clean dish towel and lay the potatoes in it, patting them all dry.

Preheat the oven to 375°F. Butter the base of a gratin pan and place a layer of the potatoes on the base. Sprinkle with salt, pepper, shallot, and garlic, and add some little dots of butter, then make another layer of potatoes. Every so often make a layer of the mushrooms. End with the potatoes, dotted with a tablespoon or

so of the butter on the top.

Pour the reserved mushroom liquid over the potatoes, then pour the cream over and finally sprinkle with the cheese.

Bake in the oven for about 1 hour, or until the top is crusty and browned. Serve sprinkled with pink peppercorns and parsley.

DAL

SERVES 4

INGREDIENTS

1½ Tbsp ghee or oil

3–4 garlic cloves, minced

2 tsp turmeric

1 small green chile, seeded and finely chopped or 2 pinches of chili powder

2 tsp ground coriander

1 tsp ground cumin

2 medium onions, finely chopped

1 cup/7 oz red split lentils

3 cups water or stock

1 Tbsp tomato paste

½ tsp sugar

salt and freshly ground black pepper

Heat the ghee or oil in large, heavy pan and fry the garlic and spices for several minutes.

Add the onion, and when it begins to brown, add the lentils.

Pour over the water or stock, add the tomato paste, and sugar, and bring to a boil.

Simmer for 40–50 minutes, until the lentils begin to fall apart.

Season with plenty of salt and a little pepper, and serve.

COOK'S TIP

For a really tasty lentil soup, simply double the quantity of water or stock used, and either sift or blend the cooked Dal.

Dal can also be made with yellow split peas, which must be soaked overnight in a bowl of warm water. Cook the Dal for about 1½ hours, until the peas are tender.

POTATOES WITH GARLIC, CHEESE, AND MILK

SERVES 6

A filling bake with a crunchy topping, consealing the creamy and tender potatoes underneath.

INGREDIENTS

2 Tbsp butter

2 garlic cloves, minced

2¼ lb potatoes

salt and freshly ground black pepper

nutmeg to taste

1 egg

1¼ cups milk

3 oz Gruyère cheese, shredded

Preheat the oven to 350°F. Thickly butter a baking dish, then sprinkle in the minced garlic.

Layer the dish with thin slices of potato cut in rounds, and season with the salt, pepper, and nutmeg.

Beat the egg and mix with the milk and pour the mixture over the potatoes so they are all covered.

Sprinkle the shredded cheese on top. Bake until the potatoes are tender and the crust is firm and golden.

WILD MUSHROOM AND CHIPOTLE SALSA

SERVES 4

The smoky scent of chipotles deliciously sets off the hearty flavor of wild mushrooms. The salsa is delicious with tacos, tostadas and tortillas, or anything from the barbecue.

INGREDIENTS

1 oz dried mushrooms or

6–8 oz fresh, including oysters, trompettes de la mort and other fleshy mushrooms

½ onion or 3 shallots , chopped

3 garlic cloves, sliced

2–3 Tbsp olive oil

1–2 pinches whole cumin seeds

¼–½ tsp mild chili powder, such as ancho

4 fresh ripe tomatoes

½ or more chipotle chile in adobo, chopped or mashed, or a few shakes of bottled chipotle

juice of ½ lemon or lime

2 Tbsp chopped fresh cilantro

salt, to taste

Rehydrate the dried mushrooms, if using, by either soaking or simmering in hot water until tender. When cool enough to handle, squeeze dry, then chop roughly. You should have about 8 heaped tablespoons of mushrooms. If using fresh mushrooms, clean and chop roughly.

Lightly sauté the onion or shallots and garlic in the olive oil, then sprinkle in the cumin seeds. Add the mushrooms, cook for a few moments, then sprinkle with the chili powder. Add the tomatoes and cook until reduced to a salsa-like mixture. Then add the chipotle, lemon or lime juice, and cilantro. Add salt to taste and serve as desired.

BONANZA BROWN RICE

SERVES 4

This rice goes very well with chicken.

INGREDIENTS

2 garlic cloves, crushed

1 medium onion, finely chopped

½ small red bell pepper, thinly sliced

2 Tbsp oil

1 cup brown rice

2 cups canned consommé

1 cup water

salt and freshly ground black pepper

Sauté the garlic, onion, and sweet red bell pepper in the oil until the onion is transparent and beginning to brown slightly.

Add the rice and cook for several minutes, stirring well.

Pour in the consommé and water, cover the pan, and cook over a low heat for 30–35 minutes, until the rice is just tender. Season with salt and pepper, and serve.

Wild Mushroom and Chipotle Salsa ▶

BROCCOLI WITH GARLIC, HOT PEPPER, AND OLIVE OIL

SERVES 4

This is especially good at room temperature, much like a salad.

INGREDIENTS

1½ lb broccoli raab (a mixture of broccoli and spinach or mustard greens)

several pinches of hot-pepper flakes

2–3 garlic cloves, chopped

¼ cup extra-virgin olive oil

sea salt

juice of ¼–½ lemon

Either steam or blanch the greens, then remove from the pan. Alternatively, you can cook the greens in a covered pan, letting them cook in their own juices.

Place the cooked greens in a pan with the hot-pepper flakes, garlic, and olive oil. Cook together, covered, for about 5 minutes.

Season with salt and lemon juice, and let cool. Serve as desired.

COUNTRY BROILED EGGPLANT

SERVES 4

An Italian-style salad of cooked eggplant slices marinated in oil and mint and finished with toasted pine nuts and Parmesan.

INGREDIENTS

1 large eggplant, sliced thickly

olive oil, for brushing

⅓ cup pine nuts, toasted

2 Tbsp chopped fresh parsley

grated zest of 1 lemon

shaved Parmesan cheese

MARINADE

½ cup olive oil

1 garlic clove, crushed

12 large basil leaves, roughly torn

1 Tbsp chopped fresh mint

salt and freshly ground black pepper

1 Tbsp balsamic vinegar

Preheat the broiler or griddle pan until very hot, then add the eggplant slices. Brush generously with olive oil, then broil or griddle until browned on both sides.

Mix together the ingredients for the marinade in a shallow dish. Add the eggplant slices and turn them in the mixture. Leave for 1–2 hours, then stir in the pine nuts. Serve at room temperature, sprinkled with the parsley, lemon zest, and Parmesan, with fresh crusty bread.

RATATOUILLE

SERVES 4 AS A MAIN COURSE OR 8 AS A STARTER

This is more of a salad, with the vegetables cooked individually, but it has all the flavors of the classic Mediterranean dish.

INGREDIENTS

about 6 Tbsp olive oil

1 large onion, chopped

2 garlic cloves, finely sliced

1 green bell pepper, cored, deseeded, and sliced

1 zucchini, yellow if possible, sliced

1 long thin eggplant, about 2 inches in diameter, cut into ¼-inch slices

2 cups canned chopped tomatoes

⅔ cup red wine

4–5 sprigs fresh thyme

salt and freshly ground black pepper

1 Tbsp freshly torn basil leaves

½ cup small black pitted olives

1⅓ cups diced feta cheese

Heat 3 tablespoons of olive oil in a large skillet, add the onion and cook for about 5 minutes over a medium heat until softened but not brown. Add the garlic and cook for a few seconds longer, then remove the onion and garlic with a slotted spoon and place in a large bowl.

Add the bell pepper to the pan and cook slowly for 4–5 minutes, then remove with a slotted spoon and place in the bowl with the onion and garlic. Add 1–2 tablespoons of oil to the pan, then add the zucchini and cook for 3–4 minutes, turning once.

Remove the zucchini with a slotted spoon and add to the bowl. Add 1 tablespoon of oil to the pan, then add the eggplant slices and fry gently until lightly browned on both sides. Remove the eggplant with a slotted spoon and add to the bowl.

Add the tomatoes to the pan with the red wine and thyme, salt, and pepper. Bring to a boil, then simmer gently for 5 minutes. Remove the thyme, then pour the hot sauce over the vegetables in the bowl. Leave to cool, tossing the vegetables in the sauce once or twice.

Just before serving, add the torn basil leaves, olives, and cheese. Serve at room temperature for the best flavor.

CHICORY ORANGE WALNUT SALAD

SERVES 4 ~ 6

INGREDIENTS

4 plump heads chicory (Belgian endive)

2 large sweet oranges

¾ cup walnut halves

3 Tbsp olive or walnut oil

1 Tbsp lemon juice

1 garlic clove, finely crushed

½ tsp sugar

Cut the chicory into ½-inch slices. Peel and slice the oranges—or divide them into segments—removing the skin and pith from each.

Coarsely chop the walnuts, reserving a few for decoration.

Mix the olive or walnut oil, lemon juice, garlic, and sugar, and pour this dressing over the combined chicory, orange, and walnuts.

Decorate with the reserved walnuts and serve chilled.

EGGPLANT AND KIDNEY BEAN CHILI

SERVES 4

Eggplants make a good alternative to lentils for a vegetable-based chili sauce. The spicing in this is quite strong—use a little less chili powder if you prefer. Serve with brown rice or tortilla chips, and an avocado dip.

INGREDIENTS

3 Tbsp peanut oil

1 large onion, chopped

2 tsp chili powder

1 tsp ground cumin

1 large eggplant, cut into ½-inch chunks

1–2 garlic cloves, crushed

1 large cinnamon stick

2 bay leaves

3 cups puréed tomatoes or thick tomato juice

salt and freshly ground black pepper

2 cups canned red kidney beans and juice

boiled rice, to serve

sour cream and fresh cilantro leaves, to garnish

Heat the oil in a large pan. Add the onion with the chili powder and cumin and cook for 4–5 minutes over a low heat, until the onion is soft but not browned. It is important to cook the onion slowly so that the spices do not burn.

Add the eggplant and garlic, and cook for 1–2 minutes, then add the cinnamon and bay leaves with the puréed tomatoes or tomato juice. Add salt and pepper, then bring to a boil. Cover the pan and simmer the sauce slowly for 10 minutes, then add the kidney beans and their juice. Continue cooking for a further 10 minutes, then remove the cinnamon and bay leaves.

Season the chili to taste, then serve on a bed of rice with a large spoonful of sour cream, garnished with cilantro.

ARTICHOKES BRAISED WITH HERBS AND OLIVE OIL

SERVES 4 ~ 6

Artichokes, stuffed with mint, parsley, and garlic, then braised with olive oil and lemon, are one of the delights of the Roman kitchen. They make a marvelous antipasto, and left-overs are delicious, too, when added to braised meats, or sliced and served with roasted fish or chicken.

INGREDIENTS

¼ cup finely chopped parsley

2–3 Tbsp finely chopped, fresh mint leaves, or more as desired

8–10 garlic cloves, finely chopped

salt and freshly ground black pepper

½ cup extra-virgin olive oil

8 medium-sized artichokes

juice of 1 lemon

Preheat the oven to 350°F. Combine the parsley with the mint, garlic, salt, and pepper, and about 3 tablespoons of the olive oil or enough to form a paste. Leave aside to marinate while you prepare the artichokes.

Remove the hard leaves from the artichokes, and cut away the sharp top from the tender, inner leaves. Pull the center open, and scoop out the thistly inside, using a spoon and a sharp paring knife.

Stuff the inside of each artichoke with the herby mixture, then lay the artichokes in a baking dish in a single layer. Sprinkle with salt, pepper, and any left-over herby mixture, then sprinkle with the remaining olive oil and lemon juice, adding enough water to cover the artichokes. Cover with a lid or with aluminum foil.

Bake for about 1 hour. Remove the lid to taste the sauce. If it lacks flavor, pour it into a saucepan and reduce until it condenses and intensifies—you want the liquid to be evaporated to isolate the flavorful oil. Once that has happened, stop boiling immediately. Season with salt, pepper, and lemon juice, then pour it back over the artichokes. Serve hot or cold.

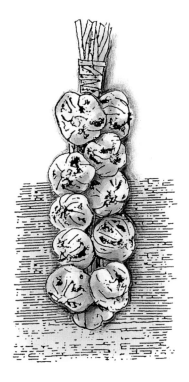

GREEK MUSHROOMS

SERVES 6 ~ 8

This meze dish is best kept simple, with the use of fresh, firm mushrooms and
a good quality olive oil for the best flavor.

INGREDIENTS

⅔ cup olive oil

½ cup dry white wine

salt and freshly ground black pepper

1 tsp dried thyme

3 garlic cloves, minced

4 Tbsp chopped fresh parsley

1¼ lb button mushrooms, cleaned

freshly squeezed juice of 1 lemon

chopped fresh parsley, to garnish

Place all the ingredients, except the mushrooms and half the lemon juice, in a large saucepan and bring to a boil. Reduce the heat and stir in the mushrooms. Cover and simmer for 8–10 minutes.

Transfer the mushrooms and the liquid to a serving dish and allow to cool completely.

Serve at room temperature, sprinkled with the remaining lemon juice and garnished with chopped fresh parsley.

WILD MUSHROOMS COOKED IN OIL WITH GARLIC

SERVES 4

This is the classic way to prepare not only porcini, but all sorts of wild mushrooms: simply with extra-virgin olive oil, garlic, and parsley. If you like, combine common cultivated mushrooms with dried exotic mushrooms in this recipe.

INGREDIENTS

1 lb porcini, wild or exotic mushrooms, or a combination

3–4 Tbsp extra-virgin olive oil and/or butter

3 garlic cloves, chopped

2 Tbsp chopped fresh parsley

salt and freshly ground black pepper

Clean the mushrooms, taking care to wipe them or trim them of any nasty bits or soggy undersides. Trim off the tough stem ends, and slice the heads and edible stems in half.

Heat the olive oil and/or butter until just threatening to smoke, then throw in the mushrooms, garlic, parsley, salt, and pepper. Toss a few times, to coat the mushrooms in the garlicky oil, then reduce the heat to low, cover, and leave the mushrooms to stew very gently in their own juices for about 30 minutes. (This is traditionally done over very low heat, for about 1 hour.)

Serve with chunks of crusty bread.

NAVY BEAN SALAD

SERVES 4

INGREDIENTS

1 cup/8 oz dried white navy beans

¾ cup Basic Garlic Dressing (page 179)

2 garlic cloves, minced

1 large red bell pepper, deseeded, and thinly sliced

2 small leeks, thinly sliced

1 Tbsp finely chopped scallions (green part only)

Cover the beans with boiling water and leave to soak overnight. Pour off the soaking water. Cover with fresh water and boil for 1½–2 hours, until tender. You may need to add more water from time to time to prevent them from sticking.

Drain the beans and, while still hot, pour over the Basic Garlic Dressing. Stir in the minced garlic and cool until needed.

Before serving, stir in the bell pepper and leeks, and sprinkle with the chopped scallions.

COOK'S TIP

Omit the leeks and scallions, and stir in 2 tablespoons of coarsely chopped fresh mint just before serving.

SPANISH ROASTED MUSHROOMS

SERVES 4

This simple Mediterranean dish of roasted mushrooms is sprinkled with fino sherry, garlic, and butter,
with a scattering of almonds, which toast while the mushrooms cook.

INGREDIENTS

1 lb large flat mushrooms

1 Tbsp fino sherry

5 garlic cloves, chopped

3 Tbsp butter

1 Tbsp chopped fresh parsley

salt and freshly ground black pepper

3–4 Tbsp slivered almonds

Preheat the oven to 400°F. Arrange the mushrooms on a large baking sheet and sprinkle the sherry, then the garlic, over the top. Dot with the butter, sprinkle with parsley, salt, pepper, and almonds.

Bake in the oven for about 20 minutes, until the mushrooms sizzle and the nuts are toasted. Serve the mushrooms immediately.

ROASTED OYSTER MUSHROOMS WITH WHOLE GARLIC CLOVES

SERVES 4

If you prefer, the mushrooms and poached garlic can be sautéed in a large heavy-based skillet,

in several batches, if necessary, so as not to crowd the mushrooms.

INGREDIENTS

2 garlic bulbs cloves, separated but unpeeled

2 cups vegetable or chicken stock

1 lb oyster mushrooms, whole but broken into clumps

6 Tbsp butter or olive oil, or as desired

2 garlic cloves, chopped

several sprigs fresh thyme

1 Tbsp chopped fresh parsley or snipped fresh chives

Preheat the oven to 350°F. Simmer the whole garlic cloves in the stock for about 10 minutes, until almost tender and the liquid has reduced by about half.

Place the mushrooms in a roasting pan. Surround with the garlic cloves and drizzle with the stock. Stud the top of the mushrooms and the garlic cloves with the butter or drizzle with the olive oil, sprinkle with chopped garlic and thyme, then roast for 20–30 minutes. If they are not done, raise the oven temperature to 375–400°F, and roast for 5–10 minutes more.

Serve sprinkled with chopped parsley or chives.

COOK'S TIP

Don't throw out the garlic poaching liquid. It is great for making soups or for adding to vegetable or meat stocks to boost the flavor.

BAKED MIXED VEGETABLES

SERVES 6 ~ 8

This light and easy-to-prepare dish is a favorite throughout Greece
during spring and summer.

INGREDIENTS

6 Tbsp olive oil

3 onions, sliced

1½ lb small potatoes, peeled and halved
or cut into thick slices

1½ lb zucchini, cut into ½-inch chunks

8 ripe tomatoes, peeled and
roughly chopped

2 bell peppers, deseeded and
sliced into rings

4 garlic cloves, finely chopped

1 tsp dried oregano

4 Tbsp chopped fresh parsley

2 Tbsp chopped fresh dill

salt and freshly ground black pepper

½ cup water

Preheat the oven to 350°F. Heat 2 tablespoons of the olive oil in a skillet and sauté the onion for 3–5 minutes, until softened but not colored. Remove from the heat.

Combine the sautéed onion with the prepared potatoes, zucchini, tomatoes, bell peppers, garlic, herbs, and seasoning in a large roasting pan. Add the water and bake for 1½–2 hours, until the vegetables are tender and cooked through, rearranging them twice during cooking. Serve this dish warm or cold.

MIXED VEGETABLE GUMBO

SERVES 4

Gumbo is a traditional dish of okra and spices from the southern states of America. It usually contains chicken or fish, but make it with just a good selection of vegetables for vegetarian friends.

INGREDIENTS

⅔ cup olive oil, plus extra if needed

2 large onions, chopped

1 red and 1 green bell pepper, cored, deseeded, and cut into ½-inch squares

1 hot chile, seeded and finely sliced

2 garlic cloves, finely sliced

1 lb okra, cut into ½-inch slices

2 cups canned chopped tomatoes

2 Tbsp butter

3 Tbsp flour

2 tsp chili powder

1 tsp ground cumin

3½ cups vegetable broth

4–5 sprigs fresh thyme

salt and freshly ground black pepper

1 eggplant, cut into 1-inch pieces

1 long, thin eggplant, sliced

Heat 3 tablespoons of oil in a large pan. Add the onion and cook gently until softened but not browned. Add the bell peppers, hot chile, garlic, and okra. Cook for 5 minutes over a very low heat, then add the tomatoes. Cover and simmer for 15 minutes.

Meanwhile, melt the butter in a large flameproof casserole, then add the flour and spices and cook over a low heat until bubbling gently. Remove from the heat and gradually add the broth, then the thyme. Return to the heat and bring slowly to a boil. Simmer the sauce for 1–2 minutes; it should be quite thin, even after boiling. Season well, then add the vegetable mixture. Cover and cook slowly for 30 minutes.

Meanwhile, heat the remaining oil in a large skillet, add the chopped eggplant and fry until browned, stirring the pieces gently so that they do not break up in the skillet. Transfer to the gumbo and simmer for a further 15 minutes.

Add the eggplant slices to the skillet and cook on both sides until tender. Season the gumbo and serve garnished with fried eggplant.

EGGPLANT AND BELL PEPPERS, SZECHUAN-STYLE

SERVES 3 ~ 4

*Szechuan cooking is very spiced. You could serve this as main course by itself,
or with a meat or fish dish.*

INGREDIENTS

peanut oil, for frying

1 large eggplant, cut into 1-inch chunks

2 garlic cloves, minced

2-inch piece fresh ginger, peeled and
very finely chopped

1 onion, roughly chopped

2 green bell peppers, cored, deseeded,
and cut into 1-inch pieces

1 red bell pepper, cored, deseeded,
and cut into 1-inch pieces

1 hot red chile, deseeded and
finely shredded

½ cup well-flavored vegetable broth

1 Tbsp granulated sugar

1 tsp rice or white wine vinegar

salt and freshly ground black peppers

1 tsp cornstarch

1 Tbsp light soy sauce

sesame oil, for sprinkling

Heat 3 tablespoons of oil in a wok. Add the eggplant and stir-fry for 4–5 minutes, until lightly browned. Add more oil if necessary. Remove the eggplant with a slotted spoon and keep warm.

Add a little more oil to the wok, then add the garlic and ginger and fry for just a few seconds before adding the onion and bell peppers with the chile. Stir-fry for 2–3 minutes, then return the eggplant to the wok with the remaining ingredients.

Continue to stir-fry until the sauce has boiled and thickened, at which stage the cornstarch will clear. Check the seasoning, adding a little more salt or soy sauce as necessary, then serve immediately, sprinkled with sesame oil, with boiled or fried rice.

GREEN BEANS WITH MINCED GARLIC

SERVES 4

INGREDIENTS

1 Tbsp vegetable oil

1 onion, finely chopped

4 garlic cloves, minced

3 large green chiles, deseeded and
sliced thinly diagonally

1 tsp ground coriander

½ tsp ground cumin

2 ripe tomatoes, blanched, skinned,
seeded, and chopped roughly

1 lb green beans, washed, trimmed,
and halved

½ tsp sugar

pinch of salt

2 Tbsp chopped fresh cilantro

Heat the oil in a wok and stir-fry the onion, garlic, and green chiles, stirring constantly, for 2 minutes.

Add the coriander and cumin, stir vigorously, and add the chopped tomatoes and beans. Stir and cover the wok for 5 minutes.

Remove the cover, add the sugar and a little salt, and stir again for 1 minute. Add the cilantro, stir for 30 seconds, and transfer to a warm serving dish.

SHIITAKE MUSHROOM, TOFU, AND ONION SKEWERS

SERVES 4

This makes a good appetizer or a vegetarian main course served on a pile of rice pilaf. It's delicious served at room temperature, too, so toss some on the barbecue when you are having a cook-out.

INGREDIENTS

6–8 fresh shiitake mushrooms, quartered

2 oz tofu, cut into bite-sized chunks

3–4 onions, cut into bite-sized chunks

5 garlic cloves, chopped

3–5 Tbsp soy sauce

1 Tbsp lime or lemon juice

several shakes of Tabasco sauce

2 Tbsp sesame oil

½ tsp ground cumin

¼ tsp ground coriander

1 Tbsp shredded or finely chopped fresh ginger root

several pinches Chinese five-spice powder

3 Tbsp vegetable oil

Soak the bamboo skewers in cold water for 30 minutes; this helps keep them from burning.

Place the shiitake mushrooms, tofu, and onions in a shallow, non-metallic pan and sprinkle with the remaining ingredients, turning everything so that it is completely coated with the various flavors. Leave to marinate for at least 30 minutes, preferably overnight, turning several times.

Thread the mushrooms, tofu, and onion onto each skewer, then cook over medium heat on the barbecue. Serve hot or at room temperature.

EGGPLANT AND LENTIL SALAD

SERVES 4

An excellent winter salad as an alternative to coleslaw—filling and tasty.

INGREDIENTS

3 Tbsp sesame seeds

5 Tbsp olive oil

I large onion, finely chopped

I tsp ground cumin

1–2 garlic cloves, minced

I large eggplant, diced

½ cup orange lentils

2 cups canned chopped tomatoes

I cup vegetable or chicken broth

salt and freshly ground black pepper

I Tbsp freshly chopped mint

Heat a large pan over a medium heat, then add the sesame seeds and dry fry for 2–3 minutes, stirring constantly, until evenly toasted. Transfer to a plate.

Heat 3 tablespoons of the oil in the pan. Add the onion and cumin and cook until starting to brown, then add the garlic and eggplant, and continue to cook for 2–3 minutes. Add the lentils, chopped tomatoes, broth, and seasoning. Bring to a boil. Cover and simmer for 30 minutes. Season and leave to cool.

Add the toasted sesame seeds and chopped mint to the mixture, then stir in the remaining olive oil. Cool the salad for about 30 minutes before serving. Do not serve too cold, or the full flavor will be lost.

PAN-COOKED BLACK MUSHROOMS

SERVES 4

So simple—a pan of mushrooms is cooked with garlic and olive oil or butter, with nuggets of scallion, and just enough juices to dip into it with grainy whole wheat bread. This makes a breakfast to wake up to, and a lovely supper, too.

INGREDIENTS

I lb flat black mushrooms

3–5 garlic cloves, chopped

2 Tbsp olive oil or butter, or more as desired

sea salt

3–4 scallions, thinly sliced

Place the mushrooms in a large skillet, black gill sides up, and sprinkle the open caps with the garlic.

Drizzle the olive oil or add the butter to the pan, letting some melt into the pan and brown the mushroom bottoms and some sink into the mushroom gills. When the mushrooms are lightly browned on the skin side, sprinkle with sea salt, turn over, and cook on the other side.

Add the scallions and continue to cook gently over medium–low heat, until the mushrooms are just tender and slightly juicy. Serve immediately.

COOK'S TIP

Serve the pan-browned mushrooms and their juices on a bed of broken up fresh naan (or warmed naan or other flat bread), and let the juices soak up into the flat bread. Serve with shavings of Parmesan or pecorino scattered over the top.

GLAZED GARLIC NEEPS

SERVES 4

This is very good with most roast meats, particularly beef and ham.

INGREDIENTS

2 heads garlic (about 25 cloves), unpeeled

3½ cups/1 lb young turnips, quartered

⅔ cup water

4 Tbsp butter

1½ Tbsp sugar

salt and freshly ground black pepper

1 Tbsp finely chopped parsley, to serve

Separate the garlic cloves. Blanch them in boiling water for 5 minutes, drain, and peel.

Put the garlic, turnips, water, butter, sugar, and a little salt and pepper into a heavy saucepan and cook gently in a covered pan for about 20 minutes, until the garlic and turnips are tender, but not mushy. If by then the liquid has not evaporated to a syrupy glaze, uncover the pan and quickly boil off the excess.

Check the seasoning and serve, sprinkled with the parsley.

SAMOSAS

MAKES 12

INGREDIENTS

4 Tbsp ghee or butter, melted

1 onion, chopped

1 tsp coriander seeds, ground

1 tsp fresh ginger root, chopped

2 cups/8 oz potatoes, boiled and diced but not soft

½ cup/4 oz peas

1 tsp garam masala

salt

2 Tbsp water

PASTRY

2¼ cups all-purpose flour

salt

5 tsp ghee or butter, melted

4 Tbsp yogurt

vegetable oil for frying

Make the filling. Heat the ghee in a skillet and fry the onions until they are soft. Then add the coriander and ginger.

Add the potatoes and peas, and cook on a low heat for 5 minutes.

Add the garam masala and salt to taste, and cook until all of the moisture has evaporated.

Make the pastry. Sift together the flour and salt and add the melted ghee and yogurt.

Knead into a soft, smooth dough, cover with a cloth, and leave to stand for 35 minutes.

Knead again and then break up the dough into small round balls.

Roll out each ball on a floured board, making rounds the size of saucers. Cut each round in half.

Moisten the straight edges of the rounds with water and shape them as cones. Place 2 teaspoons of the filling on each half round, moisten the other edges, and seal well.

Deep fry until they are golden.

EGGPLANT À LA GRECQUE

SERVES 4 ~ 6

A marinated eggplant salad with mushrooms and chopped parsley. Serve with lots of bread to mop up the delicious juices.

INGREDIENTS

1 large eggplant, sliced

about ½ cup olive oil

salt and freshly ground black pepper

1–2 garlic cloves, minced

8 oz white mushrooms, sliced

2–3 Tbsp chopped fresh parsley

Preheat the broiler. Arrange the eggplant slices in the pan and brush with olive oil. Broil until browned, turning occasionally.

Place the eggplant slices in a serving dish and add enough oil to moisten, but not so much that they are swimming in it. Season well, add the garlic, mushrooms, and parsley and stir gently. Leave in the refrigerator for 1–2 hours, then serve at room temperature for best flavor.

WARM CHICKEN LIVER SALAD WITH GARLIC CROUTONS

SERVES 4 ~ 6

INGREDIENTS

3 Tbsp olive oil

2 garlic cloves, minced

1 Romaine or iceberg lettuce torn into bite-sized pieces

8 oz fresh young spinach leaves, torn into bite-sized pieces

6 strips streaky bacon, cut into ½-inch pieces

12 oz chicken livers

3 slices white bread cut into ½-inch cubes

2 tsp sugar

1 Tbsp Garlic Vinegar (page 169) or wine vinegar

1 Tbsp finely chopped chives

Put the oil and garlic into a skillet and leave to infuse. Combine the lettuce and spinach in a salad bowl or in individual serving bowls and then leave to one side.

In another pan, fry the bacon until crisp, drain on absorbent paper towel and keep warm.

Fry the chicken livers in the bacon fat for about 5 minutes or until firm and well browned on the outside, but still slightly pink in the middle. Drain and keep warm.

Fry the bread cubes in the garlicky oil until golden and crisp. Drain and keep warm.

Heat the bacon fat, and add the sugar and vinegar. Cook gently until the sugar dissolves.

Arrange the chicken livers and bacon on top of the lettuce and spinach. Pour over the warm dressing, and serve immediately, topped with the garlic croutons and chives.

WHITE NAVY BEANS WITH GARLIC AND TOMATO

SERVES 4

INGREDIENTS

1 lb dried navy beans

4 garlic cloves

4 oz onions

4 Tbsp butter

⅔ cup tomato paste

salt and freshly ground black pepper

Soak the dried beans in cold water for 2 hours. Drain.

Crush the garlic cloves and roughly slice the onion. Soften them in the butter over a low heat.

Stir in the drained beans, the tomato paste and enough water to cover the beans by 1 inch or so. Bring the mixture to a boil, then lower the heat to a gentle simmer. (Check the water level during cooking and top up to the original level half-way through if necessary.)

Season to taste with salt and pepper when the beans are tender.

EASTERN PASTA SALAD

SERVES 4 ~ 6

A traditional combination of mint and lemon makes this dish a salad for summer. Choose your favorite pasta shapes, and serve with warm pita bread to mop up the delicious dressing.

INGREDIENTS

¾ lb dried pasta

dash of olive oil

14 oz can garbanzo beans, drained

4 Tbsp fresh mint, chopped

finely grated zest of 1 lemon

DRESSING

3 garlic cloves, minced

6 Tbsp extra-virgin olive oil

3 Tbsp white wine vinegar

freshly squeezed juice of 1 lemon

salt and freshly ground black pepper

Bring a large saucepan of water to a boil, and add the pasta with a dash of olive oil. Cook for about 10 minutes, stirring occasionally, until tender. Drain and rinse under cold running water. Drain again, and place in a large mixing bowl.

Add the garbanzo beans, mint, and lemon zest to the pasta. Place all the dressing ingredients in a screw-top jar, and shake well to mix. Pour the dressing over the bean mixture and mix well to combine. Cover, and chill for at least 30 minutes. Toss before serving.

PRESERVES, SAUCES, & DIPS

EGGPLANTS PRESERVED WITH MINT

MAKES ABOUT 4¼ LB

Try to use preserving jars for this recipe, as they make excellent presents. The eggplants must remain completely covered by the oil to be properly preserved.

INGREDIENTS

2¼ lb small eggplants

salt

2½ cups white wine vinegar

6–8 garlic cloves, according to size, finely sliced

¾ cup fresh mint leaves, left whole

1 Tbsp mixed peppercorns

2 large green chiles, deseeded and finely shredded

2 cups fruity olive oil

Cut the eggplants into quarters lengthwise, then into 2-inch chunks. Layer them in a colander with plenty of salt. Leave to stand for 2–3 hours, or overnight. Rinse thoroughly, then drain and shake dry.

Bring the vinegar to a boil in a deep pan, then add the eggplants and garlic and boil for 5 minutes. Stir once or twice, to keep the eggplants covered with the vinegar. Drain and allow to cool completely.

Layer the eggplants and garlic alternately with the mint in warm, clean preserving jars. Season each layer with a mixture of the peppercorns and sliced chiles, and pack the layers tightly by pressing down firmly with a wooden spoon.

Pour half the oil into the jars, to just cover the eggplants, then cover and leave overnight. By the next day, the eggplants will have absorbed much of the oil. Add sufficient extra oil to cover the eggplants completely, then seal the jars and leave for at least a week before serving.

GARLIC HONEY

MAKES 1½ LB

This is a useful addition to salad dressings and marinades, and for glazing pork and chicken before roasting. It is also a traditional remedy for coughs, cold sores, and acne—and hard-core garlic fanciers

INGREDIENTS

30 garlic cloves, peeled

1½ lb clear honey

Put the garlic cloves in a large, screw-top jar, and pour the honey over them. There should be about 1 inch between the honey and the top of the jar.

Cover the jar tightly and leave in a warm place for at least 1 week, turning upside down occasionally.

The juices released by the garlic will begin to turn the honey syrupy, and the goodness—and the flavor—of the garlic will pass to the honey.

◀ *Eggplants Preserved with Mint*

EGGPLANT CREAM

SERVES 6 ~ 8

Sometimes called Hünkâr Begendi *or Sultan's Delight, this delicate creamy dish is served as a sauce for meat or fish, or as a dip.*

INGREDIENTS

2 large eggplants

2 garlic cloves, finely chopped

1 Tbsp lemon juice

4 Tbsp butter

⅓ cup all-purpose flour

2 cups milk

salt and freshly ground black pepper

¾ cup freshly grated Parmesan

chopped fresh parsley, to garnish

Cook the eggplants on the barbecue, under the broiler, or in a hot oven until the skins are wrinkled and blistered and the flesh is tender, turning once or twice. Cover with a damp cloth and leave to stand for 10–15 minutes, then peel off the skin. Leave the eggplant flesh in a bowl of cold water with the lemon juice until required, to prevent discoloration.

Melt the butter in a large pan and add the garlic, then remove from the heat and stir in the flour. Cook slowly over a low heat for about 2 minutes, then put the pan to one side. Drain the eggplant and squeeze dry with your hands. Add to the pan and blend either with a potato masher or with a hand-held blender. Gradually stir in the milk.

Bring the sauce slowly to a boil over a low heat, then season to taste. Simmer the sauce for about 15 minutes, or until it no longer tastes floury. Stir in the cheese, then season again if necessary.

Pour into a warm bowl or dish and sprinkle with chopped parsley.

SESAME SEED AND GARLIC MAYONNAISE

MAKES ABOUT 1½ CUPS

Note that raw eggs, as used in this recipe should not be consumed by people with weak immune systems and pregnant women.

INGREDIENTS

2 egg yolks

2 garlic cloves

salt

2 tsp white rice vinegar

1 cup mild olive oil (or ½ cup olive oil and ½ cup peanut oil)

4 Tbsp chopped green onions

1 Tbsp sesame seeds, roasted

freshly ground black pepper

Put the egg yolks, garlic, salt, and vinegar into a blender or food processor. Mix together briefly. With the motor running, slowly trickle in the olive oil. Add the green onions almost at the end.

Transfer to a bowl. Fold in the sesame seeds and season the mixture with black pepper.

Eggplant Cream ▶

COCONUT MARINADE

MAKES ABOUT 1 CUP

This Asian-style marinade works well with firm fish, such as monkfish,

or with chicken, turkey, pork, or lamb.

INGREDIENTS

⅔ cup boiling water

3 oz creamed coconut

1 tsp lime juice

1 shallot, finely chopped

1 garlic clove, finely chopped

1 lemon grass stalk, thoroughly crushed

seeds from 3 cardamom pods, crushed

½-inch piece of fresh ginger, minced

½ tsp ground cumin

freshly ground black pepper

Pour the boiling water over the coconut and stir until smooth. Add the remaining ingredients and allow to cool before using.

GARLIC CHILE PEPPER JELLY

MAKES ABOUT 4 LB

This is a very good relish to serve with roasts and cold meat.

INGREDIENTS

4 lb sour apples

2 heads garlic (about 25 cloves)

10 small chile peppers

5 cups water

preserving sugar

Cut the apples into 1-inch chunks, but do not peel or core them. Separate and peel the garlic cloves, and cut each in half lengthwise. Halve the chile peppers.

Put the apples, garlic, and chile peppers into a preserving pan with the water, and stew for about 1 hour, until the apples are reduced to pulp. Tip into a jelly bag, or thick cloth, and leave to drain overnight. Do not be tempted to speed up the flow of juice by squeezing the bag, because this will only make the juice cloudy.

Measure the juice into a clean pan with 2 cups of sugar for every 2½ cups of liquid. Stir over a gentle heat until the sugar has completely dissolved. Boil rapidly for 10 minutes, until a little of the jelly sets when cooled on a plate, and wrinkles when you push it with your finger.

While the jelly is still hot, pour into dry, warmed jars, filling them almost to the brim. Cover the surface of the jelly with a disc of waxed paper. Put a cellophane or waxed paper cover over each jar, secure with thin string or a rubber band, and store in a dark, cool, dry place until ready to use.

GARLIC VINEGAR

MAKES 2½ CUPS

This vinegar is very handy for salad dressings and marinades for fish, chicken, and seafood.

INGREDIENTS

8–10 garlic cloves

coarse salt

2½ cups white wine or tarragon vinegar

Crush the garlic finely with the salt, and put the mixture into a large, heat-proof jar.

Bring the vinegar to a boil and pour over the garlic.

Allow to cool and then cover. Leave to infuse for 2–3 weeks.

Strain and bottle for use.

COOK'S TIP

Red Wine Garlic Vinegar—for use in strongly flavored marinades like those for stewing beef, pot roasts, and game—is made by saving red wine bottle ends and letting them "turn." Use 10 cloves of garlic to 2½ cups of the liquid, and warm the vinegar until hand hot before pouring it over the crushed garlic.

ROAST TOMATO AND GARLIC VINAIGRETTE

MAKES ABOUT 1 CUP

Pour the dressing over broiled red bell peppers, zucchini, eggplant, and onions, or toss with pasta.

INGREDIENTS

1 large tomato

3 plump garlic cloves, unpeeled

1 tsp sherry vinegar

4 Tbsp virgin olive oil

salt and freshly ground black pepper

Preheat the broiler. Broil the tomato and garlic until softened, charred, and blistered. Allow them both to cool, then peel them. Seed and chop the tomato.

Put the garlic and tomato into a blender or food processor and mix until smooth.

Add the vinegar then, with the motor running, slowly pour in the oil until well emulsified. Season to taste.

AÏOLI

MAKES ABOUT 2 CUPS

Aïoli is simply the ultimate garlic sauce. Although originally served with shrimp, it is sensational on anything from hamburgers to Bouillabaisse. Note that raw eggs, as used in this recipe should not be consumed by people with weak immune systems and pregnant women.

INGREDIENTS

4–6 garlic cloves (though of course you can use more)

pinch of salt

3 egg yolks

2 cups olive oil

lemon juice to taste

water or light or cereal cream (optional)

Chop the garlic finely and pound in a mortar with the salt until smooth. Beat in the egg yolks.

Add the oil, drop by drop at first, then in a thin stream once the mixture is glossy and beginning to thicken.

Add lemon juice to taste, and if it is too solid for your liking, add a little water or light or cereal cream.

To stop a skin forming on the Aïoli, cover with a piece of plastic film that touches the surface.

COOK'S TIP

For Almond Skordalia, add 1 tablespoon each of fresh white bread crumbs, ground almonds, and chopped parsley and a pinch of cayenne to each cup of Aïoli, and flavor with lemon or lime juice to taste. This sauce is traditionally served with cold, cooked vegetables. For Aïoli Verde, add to each cup of Aïoli a handful of parsley, 2–3 sprigs of fresh tarragon, 2–3 sprigs of fresh chervil and ½ handful of spinach, which have been simmered together in salted water until tender, drained, and sifted or blended to a smooth purée.

◀ *Roast Tomato and Garlic Vinaigrette*

Skordalia

SERVES 4

This Greek-style garlic sauce is as much about olive oil as it is about garlic. It is actually a mayonnaise, but does not use eggs to emulsify it. Skordalia is eaten with all sorts of vegetables, crisp fish, either fried or barbecued, and hard-cooked eggs.

INGREDIENTS

2–3 large garlic cloves

large pinch of salt

juice of ½ lemon, or more to taste

1 small, freshly boiled, and tender, peeled potato, broken into several pieces, plus a few Tbsp of its cooking water

½ cup extra-virgin olive oil, or as needed

Using a mortar and pestle, crush the garlic with the salt until it forms a paste, then work in the lemon juice. Mix until it forms a smooth and creamy texture.

Work in the potato and its cooking water, then slowly work in the olive oil, starting with a tablespoon or so, and repeat until the sauce is rich and delicious. After a while, you can add a slightly larger amount at a time, and stir it in with a fork or spoon.

PISTOU

SERVES 4

Unlike pesto, pistou does not have a thickening made with crushed nuts, but, like pesto,
it is often enriched with grated, sharp, Parmesan cheese. Stir pistou into pasta, steamed vegetables,
or a Mediterranean-style vegetable soup.

INGREDIENTS

3 garlic cloves, peeled

several handfuls of fresh, sweet-basil
leaves, torn coarsely

5 Tbsp extra-virgin olive oil or
more, as needed

6 Tbsp shredded Parmesan, or to taste

Crush the garlic with a mortar and
pestle, then transfer it to a food
processor or blender, and continue to
crush it more finely.

Add the basil, then slowly add the
olive oil, working the mixture in until it
forms a smooth paste. Add enough
olive oil for it to be smooth and oily,
then stir in the cheese.

Store the pistou in a bowl or jar
with a layer of olive oil over the top,
for no longer than 2 weeks. If you
wish to store it longer, you can freeze
it for up to 4 months, but omit the
cheese when freezing to ensure that it
remains fresh.

EGGPLANT PESTO

SERVES 4

A relatively low-fat pesto with a hint of smokiness from the eggplant. If fresh basil is unavailable,
try mixing 1 teaspoon of dried basil into chopped fresh parsley instead.

INGREDIENTS

1 large eggplant

1 large handful of fresh basil leaves

2–3 garlic cloves, roughly chopped

½ cup pine nuts

¾ cup freshly shredded Parmesan cheese

1 tsp coarse sea salt

¼ cup olive oil

Parmesan shavings and basil
sprigs, to garnish

Cook the eggplant over a barbecue, under a broiler, or in a hot oven until the skin is wrinkled and blistered and the flesh is tender. Leave to cool slightly for about 10 minutes, then peel off the skin.

Blend all the remaining ingredients in a blender or food processor, then add the eggplant and blend again. Garnish with Parmesan and basil.

MARINARA SAUCE

SERVES 4–6

This quantity of sauce is enough for 1 lb of pasta. Traditionally, it is served without cheese,
but if you must, use a strong hard cheese such as Parmesan or pecorino.

INGREDIENTS

2 medium onions, thinly sliced

2 garlic cloves, minced

2 Tbsp olive oil

15-oz can of tomatoes

1 Tbsp tomato paste

1 tsp each sugar and paprika

1 tsp dried oregano

salt and freshly ground black pepper

Fry the onions and garlic in the oil until they brown slightly. Lower the heat and continue to cook for 15–20 minutes, until soft.

Add the tomatoes, tomato paste, sugar, oregano, and paprika. Cook rapidly for about 10 minutes, until the tomatoes break down.

Add salt and pepper to taste, and serve with pasta.

COOK'S TIP

Stir ⅓ cup of pitted black olives and 2 tablespoons of drained finely chopped anchovy fillets to the finished sauce and heat through for a few moments before serving.

RÉMOULADE SAUCE

MAKES ABOUT 1 CUP

Traditionally this sauce is mixed with cold cooked shrimp and served over lettuce with various garnishes such as tomatoes and olives, but it can also be used as a seafood dip.

INGREDIENTS

1 Tbsp olive oil

½ cup mayonnaise

2 Tbsp sour cream

1 hard-cooked egg, shelled and finely chopped

1 Tbsp capers, drained and chopped

1 garlic clove, minced

1 Tbsp finely chopped fresh parsley

2 chopped green onions

2 Tbsp ketchup

1 tsp lemon juice

1 Tbsp Creole mustard

½ tsp prepared horseradish

¼ tsp cayenne

¼ tsp salt

few drops of Tabasco sauce

In a medium bowl, whisk the olive oil into the mayonnaise until it is all absorbed. Add the remaining ingredients and whisk until smooth. Check the seasoning and adjust, then chill for several hours or overnight to let the flavors blend.

PESTO

SERVES 4-6

Although Pesto is traditionally served as a sauce for pasta, it goes well with cold meats,
broiled fish, in soup, or on salads with a little extra oil and a dash of lemon juice.

INGREDIENTS

¾ cup finely chopped fresh basil leaves

2 Tbsp pine kernels

½ cup Parmesan cheese, finely grated, or
half Parmesan and half sardo cheese

3 garlic cloves, finely chopped

6 Tbsp olive oil

Combine the basil, pine kernels, cheese, and garlic in a blender or food processor, and reduce to a thick, green, aromatic paste.

Add the oil, a little at a time, until well incorporated.

COOK'S TIP

For Walnut Pesto, replace half the olive oil with walnut oil and use chopped walnuts instead of the pine kernels used in this recipe.

UNCOOKED SALSA WITH GARLIC AND TOMATO

SERVES 4

This is a classic salsa, rich with garlic, parsley, and cilantro. For a chunky salsa, leave it as it is;
for a smooth purée, give it a whirl in the blender for a moment or two.

INGREDIENTS

3 garlic cloves, chopped

2 jalapeño or serrano chiles, chopped

½ onion, chopped

1 lb flavorful raw tomatoes, chopped

2–3 Tbsp chopped fresh parsley

2–3 Tbsp chopped fresh cilantro

salt and ground cumin, to taste

juice of 1 lime

Combine all the ingredients and taste for seasoning. It will keep for 4–5 days in the refrigerator.

YOGURT, CUCUMBER, AND GARLIC DIP

SERVES 4 ~ 6

This light and refreshing dip should always be served well chilled.

INGREDIENTS

1 lb plain unsweetened yogurt

½ cucumber

3 garlic cloves, crushed

2 Tbsp chopped fresh mint

2 Tbsp olive oil

1 Tbsp white wine vinegar

salt

Place the yogurt in a medium-sized bowl. Peel and grate the cucumber, squeezing a little at a time in the palm of your hand to remove the excess water. Stir the cucumber into the yogurt.

Stir in the garlic, most of the fresh mint, olive oil, and vinegar. Season with salt. Cover and chill in the refrigerator until required. Just before serving, garnish with remaining mint.

SALSA VERDE

SERVES 4 - 6

Green and piquant, this sauce of fresh herbs is excellent with any fish, hot or cold, and it goes well with hard-cooked eggs. Since it is so very good with shrimp, why not try it in a seafood cocktail?

INGREDIENTS

3 garlic cloves, finely chopped

1 cup finely chopped parsley

1 Tbsp finely chopped watercress leaves

1 Tbsp mixed fresh herbs, finely chopped (basil, marjoram, and a little thyme, sage, chervil, and dill)

coarse salt

4 Tbsp olive oil

juice of 1–2 lemons

1–2 tsp sugar

freshly ground black pepper

Blend or pound together in a mortar, the garlic, parsley, watercress, fresh mixed herbs, and a little coarse salt, until they form a smooth paste.

Add the oil, a spoonful at a time, and mix well after each addition. Add the lemon juice and season with sugar, salt and pepper to taste.

VINEGAR-BASED SAUCE

MAKES 1½ CUPS

In São Paulo, this sauce is used to marinate the meats in and then after cooking it is used as an accompaniment to the meal.

INGREDIENTS

2 onions, chopped very finely

3 garlic cloves, chopped very finely

3 tomatoes, peeled, deseeded, and chopped very finely

¼ tsp sugar

6 Tbsp chopped fresh parsley

4 Tbsp chopped fresh cilantro

1 cup white wine vinegar

salt and freshly ground black pepper

Combine all the ingredients, with salt and pepper to taste. Serve in a small bowl, so people help themselves.

Set aside or store in the refrigerator before serving to allow the flavors to penetrate.

GARLIC BUTTER

INGREDIENTS

½ cup butter, softened

3–6 garlic cloves, unpeeled

salt and freshly ground black pepper

Cream the butter. Blanch the garlic in boiling water for 1 minute, drain and peel. Crush the garlic to a fine paste with a pinch of salt and mix in the butter. Season and chill.

VARIATIONS

Parsley Garlic Butter

Add 1½ tablespoon of chopped fresh parsley.

Herb and Garlic Butter

Add 1½ tablespoon of chopped fresh mixed herbs.

Mustard Garlic Butter

Add 1 tablespoon of mild French mustard.

Chili Garlic Butter

Add chili powder to taste and 2 teaspoons of tomato paste.

CLARIFIED GARLIC BUTTER

MAKES ½ CUP

This butter can be used for frying, especially potatoes, and can be brushed over pastry before baking, and over cooked buns and bagels before heating. It is also particularly good with vegetables, such as asparagus and artichokes.

INGREDIENTS

3–6 garlic cloves, unpeeled

½ cup/4 oz butter

salt and freshly ground black pepper

Blanch the unpeeled garlic in boiling water for 1 minute. Drain and peel them.

Slice the garlic, and heat gently for 5 minutes in the butter with a little salt and pepper to season.

Skim the butter and strain it through a piece of cheesecloth or a very fine sieve. Keep covered in the fridge until needed.

BASIC GARLIC DRESSING

A basic garlic dressing makes an interesting change from a normal vinaigrette. It is best served with a crisp, fresh salad, but goes equally well into cold pasta for a quick and easy supper dish. For variations to the basic ingredients, see the Cook's Tip below.

INGREDIENTS

1–2 garlic cloves, minced

1 tsp sugar

2 Tbsp wine vinegar or Garlic Vinegar (page 169)

6 Tbsp olive oil

salt and freshly ground black pepper

Combine all the ingredients in a screw-top jar, cover and shake well. Adjust seasoning before serving.

If you like, add fresh or dried herbs to taste depending on what you are serving the dressing with.

COOK'S TIP

Replace the oil with sour cream or yogurt, and the vinegar with lemon juice (the cream version is excellent with 1 tablespoon of freshly grated horseradish added to it).

Add 1 teaspoon of mild French mustard. This dressing is especially good served over warm green beans

COOKED TOMATO SAUCE

MAKES 4½ PINTS

This tomato and pepper sauce can be served with broiled fish or thinned with stock for soup.

INGREDIENTS

2 tsp cumin seeds

3 lb fresh or canned tomatoes, diced

⅓ cup vegetable oil

2–3 small to medium-sized onions, peeled and chopped

4–6 garlic cloves, chopped

1 Tbsp dried oregano, crumbled

2–3 small hot dried chiles, crumbled, or 1 large mild green chile, roasted, skinned, and diced

1 green bell pepper, roasted, skinned, and diced

salt

2–4 Tbsp chopped fresh cilantro (optional)

Toast the cumin seeds in an ungreased, heavy pan until fragrant, then crush coarsely. Set aside. Purée the tomatoes and set aside.

In the oil, fry the onions and garlic until softened, then add the cumin seeds, oregano, chiles, green bell pepper, and puréed tomatoes.

Simmer, stirring often, for about 45 minutes or until the sauce is richly flavored and thickened. Season with salt to taste and add cilantro if wished.

CONCENTRATED TOMATO SAUCE

This rich sauce can be served with pasta as it is, or with ground meat and liquid added. It is delicious poured over chicken pieces or fish steaks before baking, or used to top homemade pizza. It will also flavor soups and stews, and it is an excellent relish for cold meats, hamburgers, and frankfurters.

INGREDIENTS

2 medium onions, finely chopped

2–3 garlic cloves, minced

2 Tbsp olive oil

3 Tbsp tomato paste

3 Tbsp wine or water

1 tsp dried oregano

1 tsp paprika

1 tsp sugar

salt and freshly ground black pepper

Fry the onions and garlic in the oil until they begin to brown. Turn down the heat and simmer, covered, for 10–15 minutes or until softened.

Add the tomato paste, wine or water, oregano, paprika, and sugar.

Season with salt and pepper to taste.

Allow the sauce to bubble for 5 minutes, stirring constantly, and then serve.

DRINKS &
DESSERTS

LHASSI WITH A BANG

SERVES 2

*Traditionally served with hot food to soothe the palate, this version
will take your guests by surprise!*

INGREDIENTS

1¼ cups Greek yogurt

½ cup ice water

1 large garlic clove, finely chopped

pinch of salt

1 Tbsp coarsely chopped fresh mint

sprigs of mint, to serve

Stir the ingredients together. Serve in two chilled, old-fashioned glasses, garnished with sprigs of mint.

GARLIC BLOODSHOT

SERVES 4 ~ 6

*A cross between a Bloody Mary and a Bullshot, this is recommended
for Sunday brunch or a hangover.*

INGREDIENTS

¾ cup vodka

¾ cup chilled consommé or beef bouillon

1¼ cups chilled tomato juice

3 tsp garlic juice

1 tsp sugar

juice of half a lemon

1 tsp Worcestershire sauce

salt and cayenne pepper

Stir the ingredients together in a glass jug. Season with salt and cayenne pepper to taste, and serve poured over ice in tall glasses.

GARLIC MULL

SERVES 4 ~ 6

This is a marvelously warming drink to serve on a chilly evening. Keep the saucepan
on the go and top up your glass when you are ready for the next one!

INGREDIENTS

1 bottle robust red wine

½ lemon, thickly sliced

small orange, stuck with 6 cloves

1 Tbsp brown sugar

3-inch piece of stick cinnamon, bruised

6 unpeeled cloves of garlic, bruised

glass of port or brandy (optional)

little grated nutmeg, to serve

Heat all the ingredients very slowly in a large, heavy saucepan to just below boiling point. Use equal quantities of water and wine if you want the drink to go further.

Strain into mugs or thick glasses and top with a pinch of grated nutmeg.

MARGARITA MIA

SERVES 2

Adding garlic to this classic drink gives it an interesting twist.

INGREDIENTS

½ garlic clove

salt

4 Tbsp tequila

1½ Tbsp fresh lime juice

2 tsp Cointreau

crushed ice

Bruise the garlic and rub the cut side of the clove round the rims of two standard 3½ oz cocktail glasses.

Dip the rims of the glasses in salt and chill them in the refrigerator.

Shake the tequila, lime juice, and Cointreau together with ice in a screw-top jar and strain—so that the ice doesn't dilute the drink—into the prepared glasses.

GARLIC VODKA

MAKES 2½ CUPS

Kick-start the evening with this powerful drink, and continue the theme by serving a garlic-filled dinner.

INGREDIENTS

¾ cup garlic cloves

2½ cups vodka

1 Tbsp sugar

Blanch the unpeeled garlic cloves in boiling water for 30 seconds. Drain them and then prick each clove several times.

Put the garlic cloves into an empty wine bottle, add the sugar and pour over the vodka. Cork securely and leave for 2–3 months. Taste a little and, if not sufficiently garlicky, leave aside for a little longer.

When the desired strength is reached, drain and rebottle. This will now keep indefinitely.

> **COOK'S TIP**
> Garlic Brandy can be made in the same way, but for Garlic Gin double the quantity of sugar.
> A few strips of thinly peeled orange rind make a good addition.

Margarita Mia ▶

LIME AND GARLIC GRANITÉ

SERVES 6

On its own, this frozen ice is refreshing between courses and renews the palate for the next taste sensation on the menu.

INGREDIENTS

2½ cups water

½ cup sugar

3 garlic cloves, quartered

1¼ cups freshly squeezed lime juice

zest of a lime, finely shredded (optional)

twists of lime peel, to serve

Boil the water, sugar, and garlic together for 5 minutes. Strain and set aside to cool.

Stir in the lime juice and grated lime peel (if used), and freeze, stirring from time to time, until granular but still slightly mushy.

Decorate with twists of lime peel, and serve with thin shortbread or *langues de chat*.

GREEN FRUIT SALAD

SERVES 4

Fresh green fruit salad is an ideal ending to a summer barbecue feast.
For a change, the sweet flavors are mingled with a hint of garlic,
coming from the glossy honey.

INGREDIENTS

1 large, ripe pear

1 cup/6 oz seedless green grapes

1 small lime, skinned and segmented

2 kiwi fruit, peeled and sliced

2 Tbsp Garlic Honey (page 165)

2 tsp lime or lemon juice

1 Tbsp kirsch or tequila (optional)

1 tsp finely chopped fresh mint, to serve

Quarter the unpeeled pear, remove the core, and cut the quarters across in ¼-inch slices.

Combine the pear slices with the grapes, lime, and sliced kiwi fruit.

Mix the Garlic Honey with the lime or lemon juice, and the kirsch or tequila. Pour over the fruit and chill.

Sprinkle with mint, and serve accompanied with light or cereal cream or yogurt.

GARLIC FUDGE

SERVES 4–6

The deliciously buttery taste of this classic sweet is given an unexpected bite with the addition of garlic. The strong and savory flavor it imparts actually helps to take away some of the sweetness, so if you normally find fudge to be too saccharine, have a go at this, you'll be hooked in no time!

INGREDIENTS

4 Tbsp butter

6 garlic cloves, peeled and halved

1 cup evaporated milk

2 cups granulated sugar

pinch of salt

Put the butter, garlic, evaporated milk, sugar, and salt into a large heavy pan and cook over a very low heat for 10–15 minutes, stirring occasionally, until the sugar no longer "crunches" under the spoon.

Remove the garlic. Bring the mixture to a slow, rolling boil, stirring it continuously.

Keep the mixture bubbling, stirring frequently, until it thickens and becomes a darker gold in color.

Test for readiness by cooling a drop of the mixture in a saucer of cold water; when it stays together cleanly and does not cloud the water, take the pan off the heat and leave to stand for 5 minutes.

Beat the fudge vigorously until it begins to crystallize on the sides of the pan.

Spread the fudge about ½ inch thick in a foil-lined tray. When firm but still warm, score with a wet knife into 1-inch squares. Leave to cool, and store in waxed paper or a plastic bag in an airtight container. This fudge is best eaten within the week.

INDEX

A

Aïoli — 171
Artichoke with Mushroom Lasagne — 70
Artichokes Braised with Herbs and Olive Oil — 147

B

Beans, Simmered — 112
Beef Cobbler — 111
Beef, Eggplant, and Bell Pepper Soup — 22
Beef and Eggplant Biriani — 102
Bell Peppers in Oil, Roasted — 38
Black Mushrooms, Pan-cooked — 157
Bocadillo from Santa Gertrudis — 65
Bouillabaisse — 24
Broccoli with Garlic, Hot Pepper, and Olive Oil — 142

C

Cassoulet, Shepherd's Bush — 117
Cheese and Guacamole Pizza Wedges — 40
Cheesecake Tart, Garlic — 31
Chestnut Hash — 135
Chicken Broth with Herb Dumplings, Lemon — 41
Chicken Creole — 123
Chicken, Double Garlic — 126
Chicken and Eggplant Risotto — 72
Chicken with Lemon Grass and Cashew Nuts, Fresh — 118
Chicken with Lemons and Olives, Moroccan — 129
Chicken Liver Salad with Garlic Croutons, Warm — 160
Chicken Millefoglie, Cold — 119
Chicken Moussaka — 120
Chicken and Olive Risotto — 74
Chicken with Prunes — 128
Chicken Soup with Avocado, Garbanzo Beans, and Chipotles — 21
Chicken Thighs, Korean Braised — 125
Chicken with Tomatoes — 105
Chicken Wings with Lime Juice and Garlic — 127
Chicory Orange Walnut Salad — 145
Coconut Marinade — 168
Cottabulla — 108
Crab, Papaya — 33
Crab-stuffed Mushrooms — 32

D

Dal — 139
Duck Curry, Red — 122

E

Eggplant and Bell Peppers, Szechuan-style — 154
Eggplant and Cod Bake — 88
Eggplant, Country Broiled — 143
Eggplant Cream — 166
Eggplant and Goat's Cheese Salad, Griddled — 37
Eggplant à la Grecque — 159
Eggplant Guacamole — 27
Eggplant and Kidney Bean Chili — 146
Eggplant and Lentil Salad — 157
Eggplant Pesto — 174
Eggplant and Sweet Potato Curry — 136
Eggplant and Tomato Galette — 52
Eggplants Preserved with Mint — 165
Eggs with Green Peas and Cream, Baked — 56
Eggs, Oaxaca — 54
Eggs, Scarborough — 53
Eggs Scrambled with Tomatoes, Chiles, and Tortillas — 57

F

Fish Baked with Cumin, Moroccan Whole — 97
Fish and Vegetable Casserole — 99
Floating Island Soup — 20
Fruit Salad, Green — 189

G

Ganoug Ganoug — 25
Garlic Bloodshot — 184
Garlic Bread — 61
Garlic Butter — 179
Garlic, Butter-braised — 136
Garlic Butter, Clarified — 180
Garlic Chile Pepper Jelly — 169
Garlic Dill Pizza — 69
Garlic Dressing, Basic — 180
Garlic Fudge — 190
Garlic Honey — 165
Garlic Mash — 134
Garlic Milk Loaf — 62
Garlic Mull — 185
Garlic and Mushroom Soup, Cream of — 14
Garlic Onion Soup — 13
Garlic Pasta — 80
Garlic Roulade — 59
Garlic Scones — 56
Garlic Soup, Arcadian — 12
Garlic Vinegar — 169
Garlic Vodka — 186
Glazed Garlic Neeps — 158
Gravad Lax, Garlic — 94
Green Beans with Crushed Garlic — 155

J

Jazzed Cecils — 49

L

Lamb Cooked in Foil — 107
Lamb with Eggplant in a Sauce, Sautéed — 114
Langoustines, Steamed — 91
Lettuce Soup, Fragrant — 19
Lhassi with a Bang — 184
Lime-marinated Swordfish with Eggplants and Arugula Pesto — 92
Liver and Garlic Gratiné — 188
Liver Stroganoff — 125

M

Macaroni with Wild Mushrooms and Peas, Gratin of — 79
Mammy Patties — 53
Margarita Mia — 186
Marinara Sauce — 174
Massaia Mia — 81
Meatballs with Eggplant and Tomato Sauce — 110
Mushroom-ricotta and Sausage Cannelloni — 78
Mushrooms and Barley with New Orleans Spices — 83
Mushrooms and French Lentils, Countryside Soup of — 23
Mushrooms, Greek — 148
Mushrooms, Spanish Roasted — 150
Mushrooms, Stuffed — 14
Mussels, Stuffed — 90

N

Navy Bean Salad — 149
Neapolitan Pizza — 80
New Orleans-style Sandwich — 64
Nuts, Garlic Buttered — 46

O

Omelet with Goat's Cheese Filling, Rolled — 50
Omelet with Mousserons — 46
Oyster Mushrooms with Whole Garlic Cloves, Roasted — 151

P

Pasta with Raw Tomato Sauce — 75
Pasta Salad, Eastern — 161
Pasta with Tuna and Tomato Sauce — 71
Penne with Mixed Mushroom Sauce — 68
Pesto — 176
Pesto Pizzas, Individual — 58
Piperade — 44
Pistou — 173
"Pistou" Soup, Green — 16
Pork with Braised Mushrooms, Rosemary-roasted — 116
Pork and Eggplant Chop Suey, Spiced — 113
Pork and Red Chile Burritos — 112
Potato Streamers — 61
Potato and Tomato Gratin — 132
Potatoes with Garlic, Cheese, and Milk — 139
Potatoes and Mushrooms, Gratin of — 138
Pumpkin, Savory Roasted — 132

Q

Quenelles with Pink Fennel Sauce — 89

R

Rabbit Casseroled in Red Wine — 108
Ratatouille — 145
Ravioli — 77
Red Beans and Rice with Tasso and Andouille — 82
Red Mullet with Garlic — 93
Rémoulade Sauce — 175
Rice, Bonanza Brown — 140
Root Vegetables, Oil-roasted — 134

S

Salsa with Garlic and Tomato, Uncooked — 176
Salsa Verde — 177
Salt Cod Fritters with Garlic — 98
Samosas — 158
Seafood with Mint, Garlic, and Chives, Stir-fried — 96
Sesame Seed and Garlic Mayonnaise — 166
Shepherd's Pie — 115
Shiitake Mushroom, Tofu, and Onion Skewers — 156
Shrimp Bake — 93
Shrimp, Honey Garlic — 94
Shrimp Pancakes — 34
Skordalia — 172
Smoked Haddock Lasagne — 87
Snail Buns — 28
Sole, Tandoori — 91
Spaghetti with Eggplant and Zucchini — 69
Spaghetti with Tomato and Clam Sauce — 76
Swordfish, Middle Eastern-style Broiled — 95

T

Tapenade, Garlic — 50
Taramasalata — 29
Tarte Marie-odile — 31
Tomato and Basil Bruschetta, Ripe — 41
Tomato-Chile Eggs — 48
Tomato and Garlic Vinaigrette, Roast — 71
Tomato and Green Bell Pepper Gazpacho — 26
Tomato Sauce, Concentrated — 181
Tomato Sauce, Cooked — 181
Tomatoes with Olive Oil, Garlic, and Basil, Roasted — 28
Tomatoes, Sherbet — 33
Tuna and Eggplant Kabobs — 86
Thanksgiving Mole — 124

V

Vegetable Gumbo, Mixed — 153
Vegetable Soup, Classic Greek — 18
Vegetables, Baked Mixed — 152
Venison Sausage and Eggplant Casserole — 106
Vinegar-based Sauce — 178

W

White Beans and Porcini, Creamy Purée of — 17
White Navy Beans with Garlic and Tomato — 160
Wild Mushroom and Chipotle Salsa — 140
Wild Mushroom Soup, Basque — 25
Wild Mushrooms Cooked in Oil with Garlic — 149

Y

Yogurt, Cucumber, and Garlic Dip — 177